ONLY TO BE OPENED

BY THOSE WHO

Believe

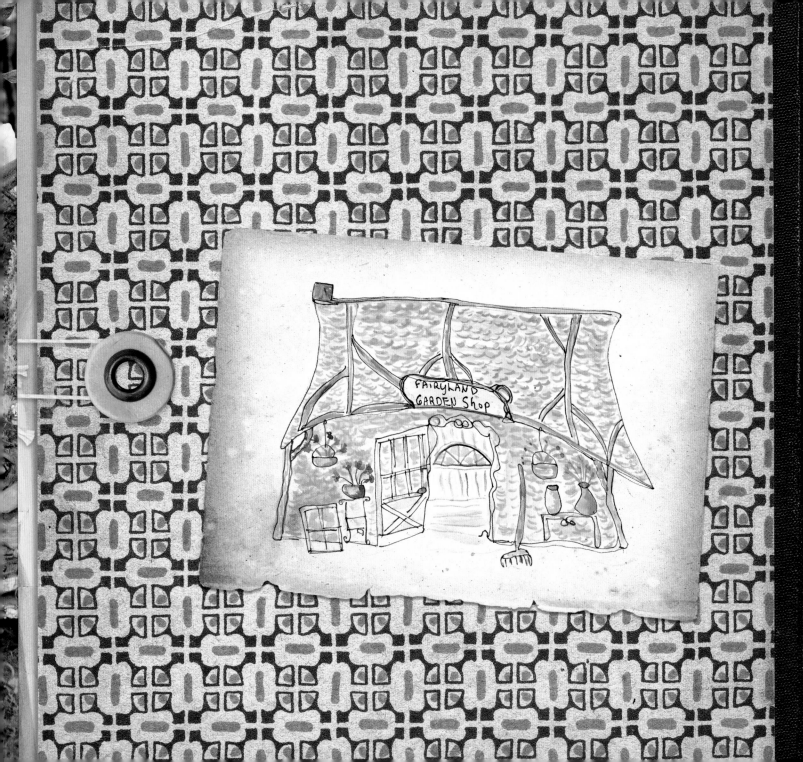

The birds were
trying to tell us
something . . .

Published by Familius LLC, www.familius.com

Familius books are available at special discounts for bulk purchases, whether for
sales promotions or for family or corporate use. For more information, contact
Familius Sales at 559-876-2170 or email orders@familius.com.

Library of Congress Cataloging-in-Publication Data
2017942642   ISBN 9781945547386

Printed in China

Edited by Laurie Duersch
Cover and book design by David Miles
Author photo by Angie Felice

10 9 8 7 6 5 4 3 2 1

First Edition

FAIRY · VILLAGE

MIKE & DEBBIE SCHRAMER

BESTSELLING AUTHORS OF *FAIRY HOUSE*

THIS SPACE FOR WRITING MESSAGES.

13126

MADE IN U.S.A.

Dedicated to children
everywhere and their
pursuit of happiness,
and to those who are
older who love being a
child at heart.

Mike
and
Debbie

POST CARD

PLACE
STAMP HERE

DOMESTIC
ONE CENT

FOREIGN
TWO CENTS

THIS SPACE FOR ADDRESS ONLY.

CONTENTS

INTRODUCTION

IN WHICH TWO HUMANS ARE INVITED TO TOUR THE FAIRY WORLD

Imagine, if you will, an extraordinary encounter with an amazing fairytale world, a fairy village tucked deep in the most awe-inspiring forest of giant trees and ferns. Moss and pine needles carpet the forest floor. Lovely shadows hide a fascinating, unseen world lit by brilliant shafts of light, revealing a mysterious curiosity.

It all began one day on a hike we had planned for quite some time to sketch and photograph a forest we had visited before but whose more arduous trail we had not yet ventured on. Our backpacks were filled with our camera, sketchbooks, binoculars, and sandwiches. It was a perfect April afternoon with gentle breezes and a welcoming bit of warmth. As we walked along the moss-laden path, our conversations turned to the beauty of the forest; we pointed out delicate leaves and lovely shafts of sunlight coming through the tall trees. The lush vegetation, beautiful blue skies, and billowy clouds were so inspiring and lovely to us. We could feel our spirits becoming calmer and remarked how happy we felt in this beautiful, peaceful place, wishing it could be our home.

We were well on our way, beyond the voices of other humans, when we began to hear the sounds of birds off the trail in the distance. Their songs were beautiful but somehow curious. When we came upon them, they were not frightened nor did they fly away; they began chirping, which, by now, sounded like a conversation. It was such a spectacle that we pulled out our camera to photograph them.

As we grew closer, the birds flew amongst themselves in circles, hopping from branch to branch, all while talking to one another with great excitement. We had never encountered such jabbering and chattering amongst a group of birds. As we photographed them, they began to fly around us in what

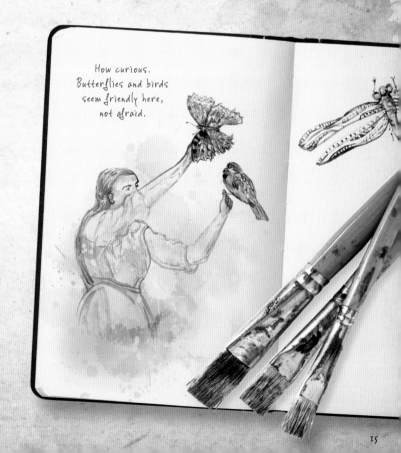

How curious. Butterflies and birds seem friendly here, not afraid.

The elf's clothes were beautifully stitched and incredibly delicate.

seemed like an effort to get our attention. We offered them bits of bread, but they showed little interest. We were curious as to the source of their exuberance, but then we realized the birds were trying to tell us something. We decided to follow them as they flew to a small hill beyond where we stood. As we reached the top of the hill, we found, to our surprise, the loveliest patches of flowers growing in circles and shafts of sunlight in what otherwise had been a shaded forest. We photographed the colorful flowers, as they were unlike any we had ever seen.

Freeing our attention from the curious flowers, we noticed the birds had flown away from us again, this time toward a large patch of sunlight above a beautifully moss-laden meadow. We reached the meadow and found that, for the first time, the birds had stopped their chattering and had perched themselves quietly in the tree above us. It was as if they wanted us to notice something. We were still musing at this odd turn of events but had decided to rest on the soft, mossy ground when we noticed the most amazing sight right near our feet. There, under a beautiful fern, sat a tiny cart, no bigger than the size of a child's hand. The little cart was made of twigs and moss with tall sides, a long handle, and curious, tiny wheels. Inside were little tools, crates, and cloth pouches, all snugly fit and tied with rope. We were so astonished that we were not sure what to think. Who would have left this tiny cart here, so unprotected in the forest, though shaded by a large, thick fern? Had someone made the cart and left it as a gift, or were they using it on a journey somewhere? Or did someone really small make the little cart? We did not know, and our questions seemed unanswerable.

The birds still sat quietly above us in the tree with a curious silence as if they knew something was about to happen. Suddenly we heard a tiny voice coming from the direction of the little cart. We turned to discover the most astonishing sight we had ever witnessed! It was a tiny person, a man, just a little taller than the mysterious cart. He seemed to be speaking to us. His voice was so small; we leaned closer and could see that

The elf's little cart he left for us to find.

The elf's fairy wife was as kind as the elf himself.

he was an elf! We almost thought we were dreaming until he began to talk, explaining he had left the little cart for us to see.

"Why did you want us to find the cart?" we asked. "We have always thought that elves didn't want to be found."

The little man smiled and remarked, "Every elf is given one chance in his lifetime to meet someone from the human world and share something about the forest with them. The birds told me you were friends of the forest, so I wanted to meet you. I set my little cart out under the fern to see what you would do."

We were so amazed; we weren't quite sure what to say to the little man. He told us we had shown great concern for his cart, which he was gladdened by, and he felt assured he could speak to us.

Our conversation continued as we learned more about the little elf's life in the forest. He told us about the village where he and his forest friends lived. He then introduced us to his wife, a kind little fairy who was traveling with him on a special journey. They had been sent to the outer boundaries of the fairy village to find land for a new village to be built. He couldn't take us to meet any of the other elves and fairies, but he could show us a place where we could view the village from a distance, make some sketches, and photograph the goings-on with our camera. The elf and his fairy wife explained that we mustn't try

to walk into the fairy village, as it would disappear and blend itself into the trees. He hoped that we would document his world with care through our drawings and photographs and share them with others so they would know to be gentle with the forest and those who live there.

Our conversation lasted well into the afternoon, then we sadly said our goodbyes. We watched the little couple disappear quietly down the path, pulling their cart behind them. As we stood listening to the gentle breeze, we were astonished at what we had just experienced but were filled with a wonderful feeling of gratitude. The little couple had shared with us something very special about their world, and we were excited to learn more. The following stories, photographs, journal memories, and sketches are what we have brought back from that day to share with you. We hope that you will delight in the gentleness of these charming little folks and their enchanted, beautiful world. ❧

Mike and Debbie

THE VILLAGE MARKET

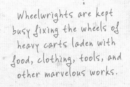

Following a path through an enchanted forest, you will discover an amazing Fairy Village. Quaint little shops with high-peaked moss-and-twig roofs, balconies, and stairways are filled with wonderful fairyland creations for little elves and fairies to buy. Any excited gnome, fairy, elf, or hobbit traveling anxiously to see the new treasures at the Village Market will come upon many wonderful wares made by the local forest shopkeepers. They will find an array of hand-sewn coats and trousers, handmade books, musical instruments, and charming little toys for the small elf and gnome children. Every day at Fairy Village is a thrilling time for the little people of Forestland!

Wheelwrights are kept busy fixing the wheels of heavy carts laden with food, clothing, tools, and other marvelous works.

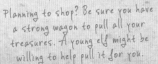

Planning to shop? Be sure you have a strong wagon to pull all your treasures. A young elf might be willing to help pull it for you.

The Village Market began many years ago as a simple fruit stand by the side of the road. Years later, it has grown into the wonderful scene it is today.

Villagers can buy most anything at the market, including delightful cups and saucers made from delicate flowers like the one shown here.

BELLTOWER

CARRIAGE WORKS

LAMPLIGHTER'S TOWER

GARDEN SHOP

ELFIN EDIBLES

For merchants traveling in from out of town, a carriage helps transfer goods and wares for sale.

VILLAGE MARKET STANDS

The Village Market is a wonderful place for all the little people of Forestland to enjoy each other's friendships and feel the excitement and fun of the open-air market. For a hobbit and his family traveling from a faraway land to finally reach Fairy Village, it surely must be comforting to see such a happy, beautiful place. Perhaps all the townspeople are busy working in their shops, for there is no one to be seen!

Far atop nearby hills, villagers can see the magical shops and shopkeepers waiting to share exciting treasures from their little markets and stalls.

Travelers come from miles around to see the incredible craftsmanship on display.

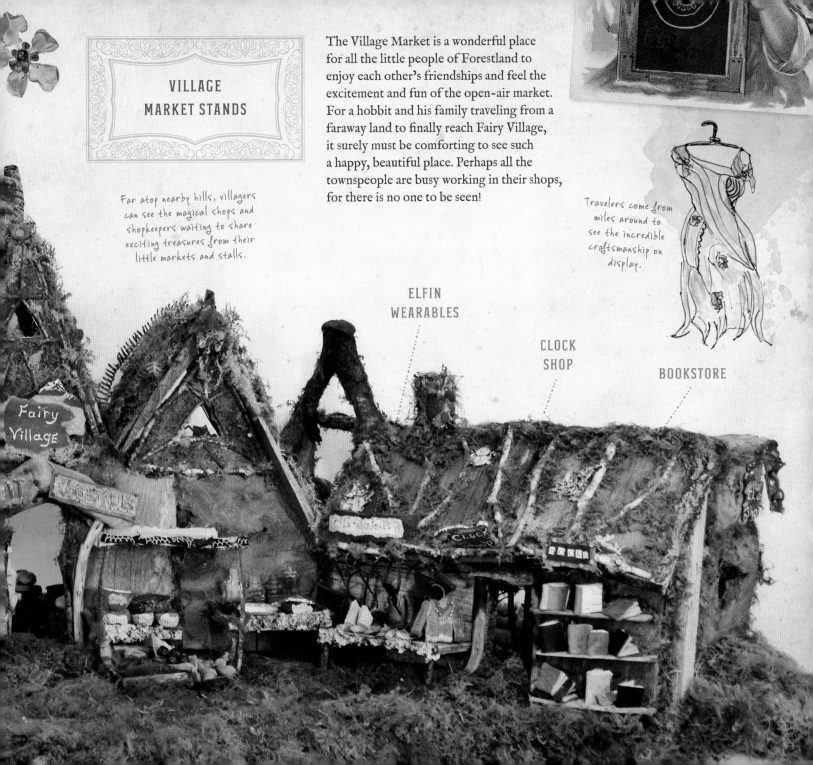

ELFIN WEARABLES

CLOCK SHOP

BOOKSTORE

Fairy Village

VEGETABLES

23

Visitors to Elfin Edibles love how wonderfully the wares are displayed; the shopkeepers built all of the stands and tables themselves and added charming awnings for shade.

ELFIN EDIBLES

he villagers enjoy taking daily trips to the Fairy Market stand called Elfin Edibles, as much for the wonderful conversation as for the food. The foragers arrive first before anyone else to deliver what they have found and supply the market with fresh forest finds like wild mushrooms, herbs, berries, greens, and wild edibles. Gardeners also bring what they've harvested from their plots and gardens, cultivated in the forest and meadows.

Elfin Edibles also includes a colorful assortment of edible flowers. These make wonderful garnishes and are also used for medicinal purposes.

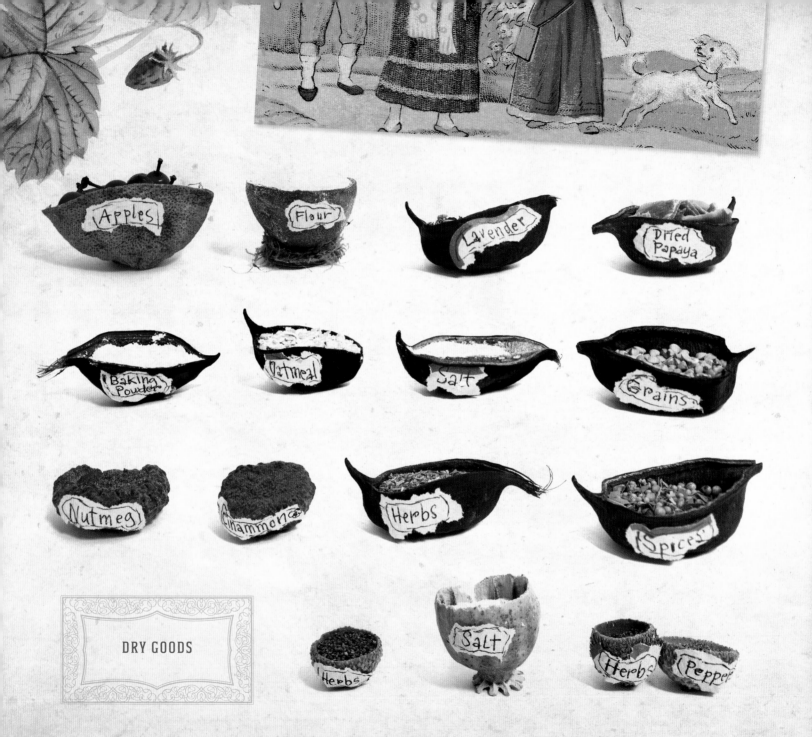

DRY GOODS

Every week, fresh berries, cherries, apples, oranges, grapes, and vegetables are displayed in large pods and open boxes for the happy buyers to peruse. The shopkeeper and his helpers are always more than happy to let the visitors try samples of any of their delightful offerings. There are also fresh herbs and spices (lavender, cinnamon, and nutmeg) as well as grains, flour, and salt—everything a busy baker or cook would need to create a delicious cake, cookies, bread, or a wonderful meal for their family or friends. Pretty, colorful glass bottles (discovered in an old house the humans left behind) are filled with oil, honey, herbal tonics, and plant extracts.

MUSHROOMS

APPLES

GREENS

ROOTS

DRIED FRUIT

Es un remedio que alimenta, forma tejidos,
fortifica, limpia la sangre, reconstituye los ner-
vios, expulsa los gérmenes patológicos, pone al
hombre en condición de trabajar sin tormento

FAIRYLAND GARDEN SHOP

The Fairyland Garden Shop is filled with pretty potted plants from the forest, gardening tools, and watering cans; there's even a rustic wheelbarrow, made by the elfin carpenter. On the little mossy hill just outside, browsers will find windows, a garden gate, a charming screen door, and even a chair and table for their own enchanted gardens at home.

FAIRYLAND GARDEN Shop

Fairies love nothing more than working in their gardens. You can be sure the garden shop is a popular spot!

ITEMS FOR SALE

Wheelbarrow

Watering Can

Garden Gates

29

ELFIN WEARABLES

The fairies may have more elaborate clothing and an array of seasonal fashions, but they do not wear them as long as the men wear their clothes. They are fond of keeping dresses and hats for many generations as pretty displays in their homes. The fairy children's clothes are the cutest. Wise fairy mothers and fairy godmothers exchange clothes they can no longer wear once a month on Market Days, both for themselves and for their children. This is such a wise thing to do and is fun for everyone, as each fairy goes home with something new and different.

A lamplighter wearing heavy boots and trousers from the Elfin Wearables stand.

Work Satchel

Work Shoes

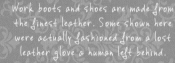

Work boots and shoes are made from the finest leather. Some shown here were actually fashioned from a lost leather glove a human left behind.

The elves, gnomes, and hobbits require durable clothing that will withstand their many hours of hard work. They look for sturdier cloth that is spun from fox and rabbit fur. They also like their shirts, pants, and pouches to be double stitched. These clothes take longer to make but last a very long time. Many of these hardworking woodsman folk report having the same pants and shoes for many years.

Work Bags

Work shirt with scarlet trim

Work shirt

Navy tunic with gold stitching

Heavy leather trousers

Leather Shoes

Leather satchel

Celebration shirt

Celebration shirt

Woven sweater for colder months

Embellished pants with gold braiding

Leather trousers with scallopped trim

BOOKSTORE

The village's library is among the best in the land, but fairies have a passion for books and insist on purchasing a few of their own. This particular bookstore was opened by a young elf who spends most of his time writing seasonal poetry. During market hours he sells the most remarkable books. After the shop is closed, he retires to his cottage where visitors might spy him rocking in his favorite chair with a pile of parchment on his lap and a scarlet feather quill in his hand. His best compositions are read aloud at village festivals, but he also enjoys sharing nonsense rhymes with the fairy children in their playhouse.

Fairies have their own authors, of course, but they love reading miniature versions of human classics, too. They are especially fond of Shakespeare and most fairies read A Midsummer Night's Dream at least once a year!

Fairies love to read. A careful look across the dwellings of Fairy Village will reveal books almost everywhere!

The Clock Shop

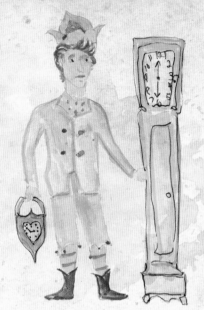

he Clock Shop is one of the most amazing shops in Fairy Village. Aside from residing on a very interesting corner of the village overlooking the beautiful valley and meadows, it is filled with intricate tiny tools, gears, coils, metal pieces, and other odd findings. The shop, where this small elf, and his even smaller elf assistant, fashion their tiny world of timepieces, has a feeling of a time long ago.

The busy workers repair old clocks and make new ones from old wood that villagers often bring to them.

LEFT: The clockmaker's work tables are always full of partially finished projects. They use various tools and clamps to fine-tune the mechanisms and gears when finishing their work.

The clockmaker created a wonderful lattice of branches and moss for the roof of his shop, giving the little workers a delightful, cool shade on warm summer days.

There are many finished clocks on shelves along the walls and a long work table where the clockmaker and his apprentice create their amazing little clocks. There is a lovely mossy green lawn right outside the workshop that little birds often visit to sing to the clockmakers as they work. There are always bits of bread for the birds each time they visit.

The apprentice's worktable

NIGHT WORK

The busy little shop becomes a quiet room filled with soft glowing light when lit by a single candle as the old elf works tirelessly into the night to finish a lovely clock for a new fairy bride. At night when his candle burns brightly across the crowded room, the clockmaker elf can almost hear the faint voices of his clocks talking softly to one another as they fall asleep in the quiet glow.

CLOCKS & WATCHES

Most of the clocks
resemble the woods
they came from—
deep dark trees with
beautiful grains or light
colored maple with
lovely golden tones.

Sometimes villagers bring old keepsakes, antiques, bits of furniture, boxes, and cupboards, requesting that the clockmakers transform their treasures into
amazing, unique clocks. Fairies, elves, and gnomes of the forest bring in bits of fine old wood they've found on their travels and ask the two timekeepers to
turn their pieces into clocks for them. It is always an exciting surprise to see the new creations at the enchanted shop of the clockmakers.

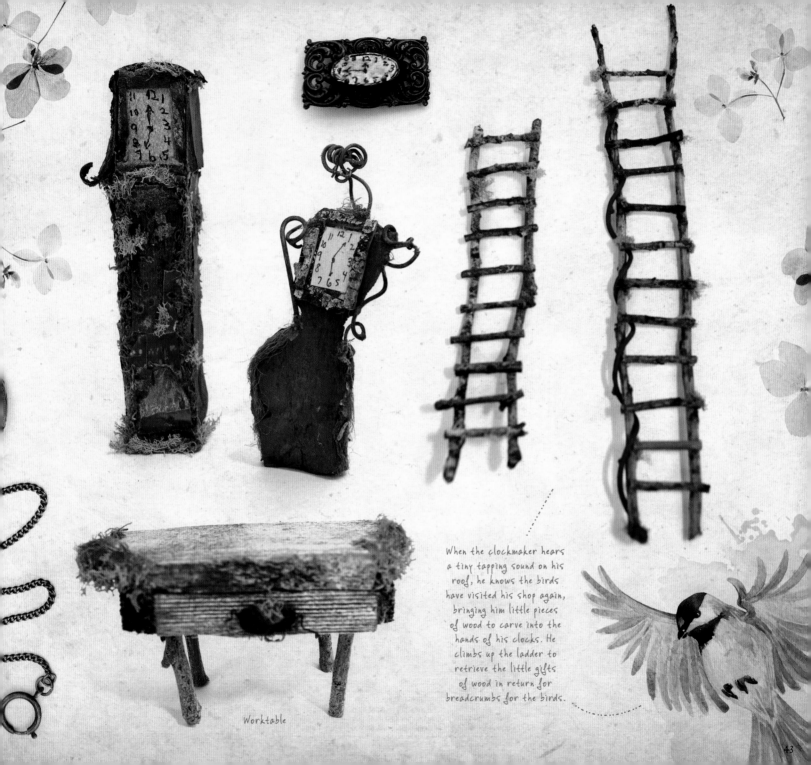

When the clockmaker hears a tiny tapping sound on his roof, he knows the birds have visited his shop again, bringing him little pieces of wood to carve into the hands of his clocks. He climbs up the ladder to retrieve the little gifts of wood in return for breadcrumbs for the birds.

Worktable

Meadowland Bakery

The Meadowland Bakery is the heart of the village; everyone says it is one of the most delightful shops in the land. The wonderful smells of warm baked bread and pastries seem to permeate the entire village, bringing a happy smile to every face. Every day at the bakery, fairies, elves, gnomes, sprites, and hobbits find wonderful donuts, bagels, muffins, pies, and even pretzels to bring home to their families or to treat themselves after a long journey into the forest. It's a warm place to work, and the smells are free and invigorating.

A cheery elfin baker.

The industrious bakers had large wooden ladles carved at the mill, which they use for stirring huge batches of dough.

The busy bakers have every kind of mixing bowl, spoon, ladle, and other kitchen utensil they need to make any imaginable baked creation.

LEFT: The cheerful pastry makers also set many wondrous baked goods outdoors on the lively Market Days. During the exciting spring celebrations and other festive occasions, long tables are filled to the brim with trays of beautiful pastries, all displayed under the lovely pavilion built by the artistic elves and gnomes. The bakers always need a few extra helping hands for those busy times, but their planning and efforts are impeccable, no matter what the demand.

Waiting for excited little elves, hobbits, sprites, and other forest people, warm and delicious muffins of all flavors line the shelves of the bakery.

The old elfin baker sometimes takes a moment on a quiet evening to cherish the gentle spirit that is in his little bake shop.

BAKERY AT NIGHT

BREAD OVEN

EQUIPMENT

The creative elfin
bakers sometimes
find inspiration in old
cookbooks foraged by
adventurous hobbits.

I. Suppen.

Man unterscheidet:

a) Fleischbrühesuppe u. Kraftbrühe mit
   Einlagen.
b) Gebundene Suppen u. Schleimsuppen
c) Wassersuppen u. andere (Erbsensuppen)

Die angegebenen Mengen sind für
4 Personen gerechnet.

Fleischbrühe.

Unter Fleischbrühe versteht man das
Kochwasser des Fleisches & der Knochen mit
den darin gelösten Bestandteilen: Eiweiß,
Fett, Extraktstoffe und Salz. Beim Kochen des
Fleisches verfolgt man 2 verschiedene Ziele.
Entweder die Bereitung einer kräftigen ge-
haltreichen Fleischbrühe oder die Herstellung
eines saftigen Fleisches.
Im ersten Fall stellt man die zerkleiner-
ten Knochen und das Fleisch mit kaltem Wasser
auf und läßt es langsam zum Kochen kommen.
Dann zieht das kalte Wasser die Fleischfaser-
zellen aus und die Nährstoffe gehen in die
Brühe über. Will man aber das Fleisch saftig haben,
so muß man es in kochendes Wasser geben,

Suppen

Fische

Fleisch-
speisen

Braten

Saucen

Gemüse

Kartoffel-
speisen

Salate

Mehl-
und
Eierspeisen

Gelees und
Gefrorenes

Einge-
machtes

Pasteten

Backwerk

Getränke

Diverses

DETAILS OF THE MEADOWLAND BAKERY

Above the warm and cozy bakery are little cottages for the old elf baker and his younger elfin assistant. Each has a small cottage to retire to after a busy day in the bakery.

Anyone who visits the bakery can watch the old elf baker and his little elf apprentice making all the wondrous pastries and breads, as the front of their shop is open for all to see. Observing the bakers mixing, stirring, and adding berries to pies, herbs to breads, and toppings to donuts will delight any passerby who loves the magic of seeing simple dough turned into an enchanting array of edible creations.

Sometimes the bakers give bread to the birds in exchange for feathers, which they then trade to the fairy seamstress to make wonderful baker's hats for them. The inventive little seamstress uses the beautiful feathers in her gorgeous, heavily embellished hats.

The baker always has a large supply of bright red apples in his shop, ready to make wonderful apple pies for anyone who wants them.

The bakery has a very special oven for making multiple pies and loaves of bread for the villagers. It was formed out of a large U-shaped piece of bark from an old fallen tree in the forest; an old hobbit brought it to the baker long ago. It must be very magical because every time the pies and breads are finished baking, the fire suddenly goes out and the breads and pies are perfect. Perhaps the old hobbit gave the bark an obliging spirit to make the oven always bake everything perfectly.

BAKERY GOODS, UTENSILS, AND EQUIPMENT

Market Day tables loaded with pies and other baked goods

Donuts (glazed and chocolate iced)

Cooling shelf

Pies (apple, blueberry, blackberry, and huckleberry)

Bagels

Pretzels

Bread and rolls

Large
mixing bowl

Medium
mixing bowls

Large mixing spoons and paddles

Water
vessels

Serving tray

Bread oven

Measuring
spoons

Spice
containers

Measuring bowls

flour

Flour

Flour (ground at the village mill)

51

VILLAGE MILL

Bags of flour ground at the mill.

 he Village Mill was built as soon as the builders were able to get water power for the saws; they then cut lumber for the mill and the rest of the buildings. The mill has a water wheel, which turns the gears inside to grind grains into flour. The elves and gnomes diverted water from the streams to power the wheels so they would turn. Once the water leaves the water wheel, it is again diverted to irrigate gardens and trees and give water to everyone in the village. Water is also turned in to the fields to create lakes and ponds for the ducks, geese, and other birds.

The mill needed to be near a stream to use water for power. The elves and gnomes were quite good engineers, as they used the natural gravity flow from nearby waterfalls.

LEFT: The elves and gnomes were especially excited to use their unique ideas for building such an important structure for the village. They worked together for many months thinking of how the mill should look, talking together and sharing ideas. Finally, they drew the plans and began building the first mill of Fairy Village.

The builders knew they wanted to have many windows in the mill for the people who worked inside. They worked tirelessly on tall ladders to build the windows up high to let more light into the mill.

Hardworking elves and gnomes had gathered many fascinating objects from their travels throughout the land over the years: metal gears, cogs and wheels, rusted metal parts and pieces, pipes, coils, hinges, and many other odd things. They didn't really know what they would do with them when they discovered them; they just knew they needed them for something important. If only the humans could see how these little builders transformed their discarded objects!

Long hours spent lifting bags of flour makes this job for only the strongest of elves.

VILLAGE MILL

FLOUR

On the front of the mill, they placed a very large, circular design made of earth colors with a blue bulb in the middle. When the mill was running, the bulb would light up to let people know to be careful approaching the mill.

The elves and gnomes made lumber for the villagers by using fanlike blades in the mill.

The builders of the Village Mill used thick bark from old fallen trees of the forest for the roof of the mill. They wanted their building to be well protected from the snow during cold winters in the deep forest. They put thick moss in between the bark to add more warmth to the roof.

Village Mill

One of the elves was a very talented artist. He loved to paint the beautiful trees and plants surrounding the mill. One day, another elf noticed him painting by the lake early in the morning before the work began at the mill. He asked if the artist would like to do a painting of the mill to display at the top of the building. The artist was overjoyed, and to this day, his wonderful painting still looks out over the lake and trees that he loves so much.

When an animal's fur is combed, it is used to spin cloth for the flour sacks. Flax and wild grasses are also spun in the mill and made into cloth.

flour

flour

VILLAGE WORKSHOP

When the little people of the forest built the village, the workshop was one of the first buildings they constructed. They built everything in the workshop for the rest of the village. The Village Workshop is used by the little people of Fairy Village in many different ways. The hardworking elves and hobbits make nearly everything out of wood and metal for the people of the village. The workshop is open to all of the villagers, shopkeepers, and those who live in the cottages. Furniture makers or clockmakers all have workshops of their own, but they visit the Village Workshop to work on bigger things that require the use of more tools. They even get their own tools sharpened at the Village Workshop.

Worker elf

ABOVE: The workshop can get crowded at times, but the elves and hobbits never look bewildered as they successfully complete all the projects they're working on, staying just as happy as when they woke up earlier that morning.

LEFT: The Village Workshop has every kind of tool imaginable for cutting, bending, and shaping wood or working with metal. The workshop builders know how to dig ore from the mountains to make the metal for the things they need.

The Village Workshop is a carriage house, a toolmaking workshop, and a place for making wood and metal wheels for wagons and carts.

The elves and hobbits trade with the gnomes from the nearby forest for coal to burn in the blacksmith area of their workshop.

SINK

CART

WORKTABLE

There are those who have many wonderful skills and are at the workshop every day, while others bring their projects in now and then to work on them. Sometimes an elf or hobbit will walk into the workshop with plans on bits of paper and later come out with a cart or a cabinet, all finished and ready to use.

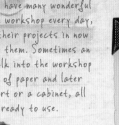

Most of the windows for the village are made by skilled craftsmen in the workshop. Thin pieces of lumber, cut at the mill, are carefully fitted together. Only skilled elfin workers are entrusted with this task.

DOORS

The gnomes brought wood from a mountain far away to make the heavy front door of the workshop and other village dwellings.

GLASS

Thin mica from the rocks inside the mountains is used for many of the windows in the village.

CONSTRUCTION

The busy workers love to tie knots to fasten things together; they are master knot makers. They often use the thick vines from trees in the forest as rope because they are so sturdy.

61

WORKSHOP INTERIOR

Bow saws

Push broom

Various axes

Shovels

Scrap wood

Screen door in progress

Saw

Tools

Scrap metal

Anvil with hammer

Cutters

Newly finished large cart wheel

Small cart wheels

Workshop sink

Cart

Ladder

LAMPLIGHTER'S TOWER

ong ago, the fairies befriended the fireflies without really knowing it. The fairies were having a summer picnic and brought their favorite tea in bottles, which consisted of herbs, fruits, and honey. When they had left the tables and were dancing in the light of the fireflies, they noticed another group of fireflies drinking from the teacups. The idea came to them to try an experiment. The lamplighter fairy put some of the tea into bowls and set them up in the lamps (instead of candles); the fireflies came to drink the tea, lighting the lamps all night.

The lamplighter appointment is for life and comes with a house in the charming, rustic little tower.

To this day, just before dusk, the lamplighter fairy continues to visit all the lamps in the village, bringing a bottle of firefly tea, his ladder, and extra bowls. He climbs up and down the ladder to fill each lamp with the special tea. It is his job to collect all the ingredients needed to keep a good supply of herbs, fruits, and honey for the lamps. The herbal tea is kept in the Lamplighter's Tower.

To be a lamplighter is a job usually given by appointment to an older person who has experience gathering herbs and fruits as well as beekeeping, cooking, and preparing medicines.

Funnel used to fill lamps with firefly tea.

Fairy Furniture Shop

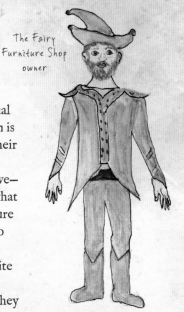

The Fairy Furniture Shop owner

The Fairy Furniture Shop is perhaps the most unusual shop at Fairy Village. The story of its construction is equally unusual, and it involves two hobbits. On their everyday travels to search for abandoned objects, these two hobbits—who were particularly inquisitive—found a very unusual treasure: an instrument, or what looked like part of an instrument. They weren't sure what it was exactly, as it obviously had belonged to one of the tall people, but they did recognize the words written on the strange object (which was quite like their own instruments). Buttons and knobs, peculiar handwriting, painted in black and gold—they knew it was something very special.

Hobbits never work alone while gathering, partly to protect themselves but also because they can accomplish more together with their combined great strength and wit. So they called upon their fellow hobbits to gather up any large wheels, pulleys, wood, hammers, saws, and other tools to make a huge cart to move the instrument.

Fairies and elves love all kinds of furniture, from the soft and delicate (above) to the rustic (below).

A beautiful fairy piano

Forest creatures often help with finding abandoned objects

Burdett

After many weeks, the mysterious object had been transported, ever so painstakingly, back through the woods to an empty field next to the village. Hobbits never make hasty decisions, so the instrument was left to be pondered upon until a creative idea came to them.

Months later, while the instrument became a curiosity to the birds, rabbits, and foxes of the field, another small group of hobbits discovered a large wooden armoire broken into many pieces on the forest floor. Perhaps it had fallen off a wagon and its owners had unknowingly trundled off through the woods toward their new home, leaving the dejected wardrobe to fend for itself.

The hobbits began to salvage and transport their amazing new discovery back to the field where the instrument patiently waited. Month after month, the hobbits hammered and sawed, carried and lifted, pulled and attached, running back to their workshops to gather even more odd and curious objects to combine with the once forlorn, discarded armoire.

After they added small, narrow wooden drawers, old wooden spigots, and a huge wooden clamp found in a human's abandoned barn, the building was nearly complete. By this time, everyone from Fairy Village had begun to gather about the serious workers with questioning glances and excited eyes. The villagers knew something wonderful was about to be revealed.

Hobbits always know when they are finished with a project; they have a sense about those kinds of things. The final thought that came to every hobbit at the same time, as they were of one mind and heart, was to add the finished piece to the top of the musical instrument. They stood back, contemplating their many months of wise ingenuity and diligent work. They were finished. They had the humans to thank, in part, and their keen eyes for discovering lost treasures as well as their wondrous ability to always work together.

The villagers were so excited to see the amazing new building the hobbits built. Everyone marveled at the imaginative way the hobbits assembled the new dwelling, but what was it going to be? An art museum for sculptures and paintings, or perhaps a new library for the hundreds of old books stored away? They all began to talk amongst themselves, as little folk always do because they are very friendly and love to listen to each other.

Elves, who can sometimes be very quiet, often break their serious demeanor with surprising wisdom. One little elf's voice broke through the tiny chatter of the crowd with a wonderful idea—a furniture shop! Fairy Village was without such a shop, so his inspired idea was received by all the villagers with wonderful delight! The hobbits all smiled, as they do when others are as wise as they. The little elf had been inspired to name the new building the forest's first furniture shop. All was well. After months of mystery, hard work, and inspiration, the villagers had an exciting new adventure to follow . . . and indeed, they did!

Burdett

S.N. SWAN & SONS

FREEPORT. ILL.

FURNITURE GALLERY

The hobbits had built the most wonderful building for the new furniture shop. On opening day, it was filled with amazing little chairs, tables, benches, stools, and armoires. The visitors to Fairy Village were so excited to see this new shop that before you could blink an eye, every piece of elfin furniture was snatched up and taken happily away to new homes. But what a wonderful dilemma for the new shopkeeper of the Fairy Furniture Shop to have all of the little furniture bought up so soon! Since fairies seem to have a sixth sense about helping others, the elfin furniture shop owner would not be at a loss for long. The fairies had made beautiful little furniture too and could bring all their lovely pieces to his shop the next morning! The fairies, with the help of their elfin friends, arrived early at the Fairy Furniture Shop and brought the most magical and enchanting pieces the shop owner had ever seen. They quickly set about displaying their lovely chairs, tables, beds, and loveseats around the rustic shop, transforming it into a beautiful, elegant dwelling.

CHAIRS & BENCHES

BEDS

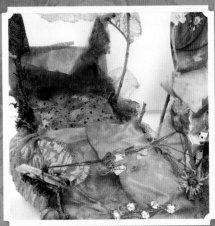

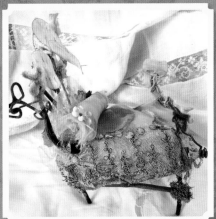

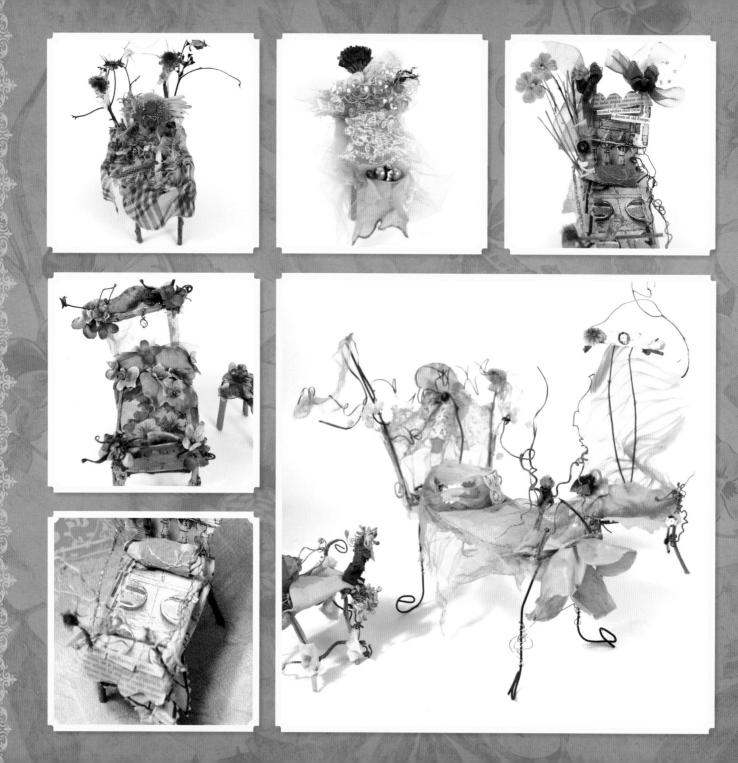

TABLES
& DESKS

VOL. 133.

fields were filled with beautiful flowers.

RUSTIC FURNITURE

ELF LIBRARY

The Elf Library is surely the quietest place in Fairy Village, as most libraries are everywhere. But in this land of fairies, elves, gnomes, sprites, hobbits, and other fairytale people, their library is quite magical. Everyone who visits this enchanted library returns over and over again to experience this mysterious place.

LEFT: The Elf Library was built by many of the elves and fairies of the forest. The elves are great carpenters, and fairies, of course, love to paint and embellish everything with flowers, leaves, and anything pretty. Little sprites are wonderful sign painters, so they were asked to make the signs for the library. Everyone worked together to create this magical place.

The large windows on the front of the library provide ample light for eager readers.

Those who love fairytales will find wonderful drawings in the library of the Mad Hatter having his enchanted tea party with Alice and the Rabbit, along with lovely pictures of rural country scenes.

The top floor has a sitting room with a cozy chair and table with wonderful drawings and paintings on the walls. You can read your book and gaze out the window, dreaming of faraway lands.

Over the years, the little library brought wonderful memories to all its readers and became part of the forest as thick ivy wound all around it.

The lower floor has shelves of old books, pages of handwritten music, and maps from long ago. There's even a soft, mossy rug for children to sit on as they read.

Each visitor added their favorite poem or story to the inside of the huge front door; some even did beautiful paintings or attached pictures of their little friends or places they had traveled to. It is a special, happy place in the forest.

THE LIBRARY DOOR

When we (as humans) go to a library, we walk through the front door. But when little people visit the Elf Library, the entire front wall opens so they can choose which room they would like to enter.

LIBRARY BOOKS

The forest library has many wonderful books for the little visitors: *The Music of Leaves*, *Earth Sounds*, *Bird Songs*, *The Fluttering Bird*, *Small Sea Life*, and many other amazing books to read.

SCHOOL OF THE FOREST

There is so much to learn about nature at the School of the Forest. The teachers know the spirit of the outdoors has as much to teach the little students as any formal teacher could and are excited to explore nature with them.

LEFT: Today's art lesson was to draw and paint from nature. The teacher asked all the little elves, fairies, and gnomes to draw what they saw on their way to school. They were excited to use their talents. As you can see, the students left some very accomplished works.

BELOW: It looks as though the little forest children learn similar things human children do. They practice their letters and read from books about folklore and the history of the forest, and we have glimpsed their talents in drawing and painting.

The children of the forest must wear shoes and boots to school, but once they arrive at their enchanted little building, bare feet are much more fun.

The map shows the islands that exist far beyond Fairy Village.

Everyone is excitedly awaiting the nature walk this afternoon! The meadow is a beautiful place where little ones can find butterflies, sparrows, squirrels, rabbits, and many other wonderful creatures.

The little students love the name of their school because the forest is their home and their favorite place to be.

Nature Walk this afternoon at the Meadow

t Lesson Today Painting Nature

School of the Forest

A B C D E F G H I J K L M

N O P Q R S T U V W X Y Z

The cozy little school has a wonderful reading corner for those inquisitive students who love books (with an abundance of books on the shelf).

Eager little learners bring their knapsacks and backpacks to school filled with paper, pencils, books, compasses, and other supplies needed to get through their busy day.

SCHOOLYARD In the front of the school is a lovely yard, a playground for the little elves, fairies, and all the other young ones. They love the slide and to play tag on the soft, mossy grass. They might paint, exercise, or just lay on the grass to watch the lovely clouds slowly pass by. Sometimes they will sit in a chair and read their favorite book or share a bench with their friends and tell stories about their exciting excursions through the forest. Other days, they bring out their harps, trumpets, and other musical instruments to play beautiful songs for all the birds and animals to hear.

The School of the Forest is quite a wonderfully quirky dwelling. Its roof, made of curled bark and moss, seems to dance about as if it were a river or the wind. An odd rustic chimney sits atop the woodsy roof; the old wood stove connected to it rests warmly in a corner of a shed inside the busy school.

Chimney

Roof

School

Through the windows at the front of the school, the students can see in to the schoolroom. They watch anxiously for their teacher to appear at the window, for then they know their lessons are about to begin.

Door

Bench

Slide

If anything breaks at the school, the teacher ties a note around a blackbird's neck and he delivers it to the elves, who arrive very quickly to mend and repair.

Gate

Every morning, the teacher rings the bell to call the children to school. It is surely the most intricate bell of any school. Made by the blacksmith elf at Fairy Village, it is one of the students' favorite things in their unusual school.

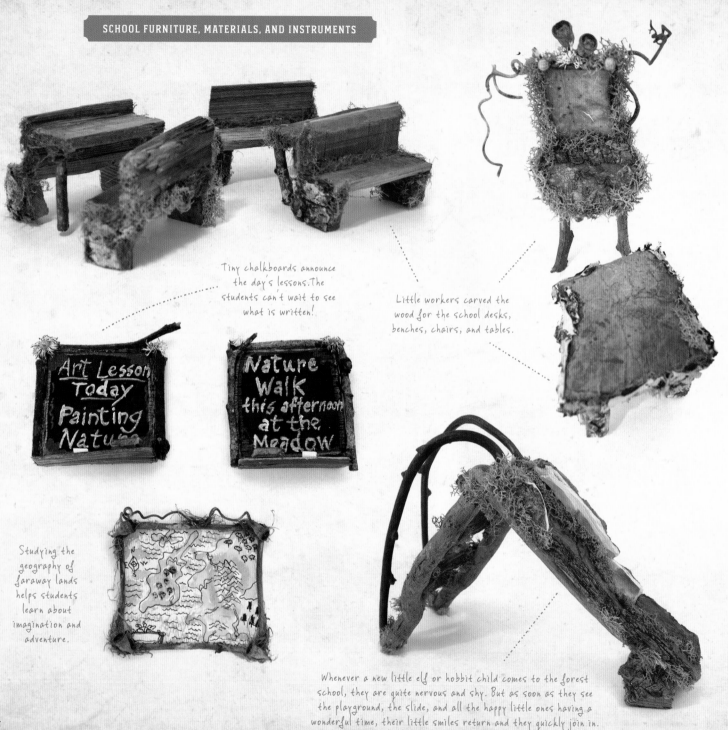

Tiny chalkboards announce the day's lessons. The students can't wait to see what is written!

Little workers carved the wood for the school desks, benches, chairs, and tables.

Art Lesson Today Painting Nature

Nature Walk this afternoon at the Meadow

Studying the geography of faraway lands helps students learn about imagination and adventure.

Whenever a new little elf or hobbit child comes to the forest school, they are quite nervous and shy. But as soon as they see the playground, the slide, and all the happy little ones having a wonderful time, their little smiles return and they quickly join in.

At the School of the Forest, there is always lots of paper to draw on or practice writing letters, as well as a fun abacus for the students to work on their numbers. The little students are never at a loss for things to do.

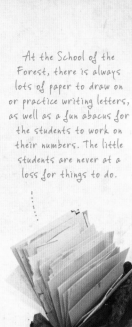

Music has always been in the lives of the young elves and hobbits of the forest, and drums are their very favorite instrument to play. The little musicians seem to have the most natural rhythm. They make their own drums by carving out logs and covering them with old leather.

An ingenious way to do sums and other figures.

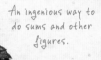

Drawing and painting class is a favorite at the forest school. Students love making paintings of creatures they find on their nature walks.

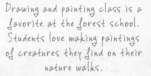

THE TEACHER'S READING ROOM

The School of the Forest is in the most beautiful, enchanted garden of the forest. Nearby, in meadows of colorful flowers, sits the wonderful Teacher's Reading Room. The little fairies, elves, and sprites love their teacher; she seems as young as they are. Always smiling, the kind teacher is like a mother to all the little forest children.

With many windows to look out from, the teacher can enjoy the beautiful gardens around her and see the fairy children playing their wonderful pretend games. It is an enchanting cottage, all her own, yet the kind fairy teacher is rarely ever by herself. Visitors come often to hear her stories, and the children are always near, their happy, sweet voices lilting through the air like beautiful flowers.

The shape of the teacher's magical room is very charming; it looks like a cottage from a fairytale.

The older elves built a wonderful reading room for the cheerful teacher in the garden by the children's school. The little ones love running over when she is there to ask for another story or poem, which the obliging teacher always shares.

THE FAIRY CHILDREN'S PLAYHOUSE

This sweet little playhouse was built for the fairy children. They love to go out and play make-believe, pretending they are humans or grown-up fairies. They imagine they can fly over the village and into the forest. They love to look at the pictures on the wall that were taken from a discarded book. The playhouse is a gathering place for younger fairies, especially in rainy weather. They love to have their fairy mothers and fairy grandmothers make sandwiches for them to take out to their playhouse for lunch with their friends.

The fairy children love to sit back on the floor, looking at the wonderful drawings on the walls of the playhouse, studying the pictures of castles, towers, and little villages belonging to the humans (whom they've never met). Such a curious life they lead, living so far from these strangers yet knowing so much about their world.

Sometimes after the fairies have run through nearby waterfalls and ponds, they skip back to the playhouse and move all the furniture outside onto the mossy lawn.

The Hatter's Toy Shop

There can never be too many toys for the little ones in Fairy Village. Fairy parents are always looking for ways to occupy their little ones. Since the very youngest fairies love to organize little objects in baskets and boxes, the Hatter's Toy Shop carries pouches of smooth rocks, little bits of driftwood, hand-carved wooden blocks, and other small treasures for the little elves and hobbits to play and build with.

Fairies love to imagine and encourage even their youngest children to begin playing with simple toys.

Fairy craftsmen worked for weeks to create the amazing hat-shaped shop with its intricate details of tassels and trim.

ABOVE: This remarkable little toy car was fashioned from dried pods, acorn caps, bark, and moss.

Fairies like different-colored textiles with interesting patterns, so quilters weave small multicolored toys out of pretty leftover fabric pieces. The fairy children roll and toss them to each other. Adults enjoy the toy shop as well with amusements like treasure hunting games. The toy shop always has games with complex instructions and detailed maps for the explorer elf or gnome to search for treasures in the forest.

GAMES

Adolescent elves and gnomes like adventure, discovery, and exploring games.

Toy boat

Toy airplane

Toy car

TOYS

Shopkeeper's ladder

Secret entrance

TOY SHOP DETAILS

BOATS

One of the fairies' favorite summer activities to do is row in little boats with their families. During these times, the fairy children like to play with their toy boats in the ponds.

CARS

Fairy children are fascinated with anything that resembles what they see in the human world, even cars and trains.

MAGICAL INSTRUMENTS

On warm days at the the Fairy Children's Playhouse, little fairies and elves bring out their harps, trumpets, and other musical instruments to play beautiful songs for all the birds and animals to hear. The best selection of instruments can be found at the Hatter's Music Shop next door.

AIRPLANES

Fairy children often see airplanes flying above them in the clouds; they are always so intrigued by these fascinating machines. Their parents do not need to invent airplanes, however, as mature fairies have their own wings with which to fly—as will the fairy children someday when they are a little older. The children were so anxious to have airplanes, they begged their parents to create some for them.

Seeing their fairy children determined to have airplanes of their own, the parents asked the toymaker to make some for the fairy children, and that he did! And as an extra surprise, the inventive toymaker constructed amazing little toy cars, just like curious human cars. The fairy children were wonderfully surprised with such delightful gifts! The toymaker received many hugs and smiles that happy day.

THE HATTER'S MUSIC SHOP

The Hatter's Music Shop is a giant hat filled with every kind of musical instrument imaginable. Fairy children are less inclined to use formal instruments when they dance and can often be found tapping on garden fences and gates with wooden sticks when outdoors and banging on pots and pans when indoors. Many of the fairy great grandparents are music teachers, however, and most fairies eventually learn how to play several instruments before they're grown.

Fairies are particularly fond of stringed instruments and enjoy woodwinds, too.

RIGHT: A magic door on the front of the hat reveals a hidden straicase leading up to the top of the hat.

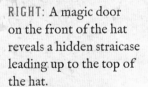

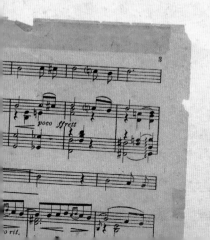

The village instrument makers pass on their craft to their sons and daughters.

MUSIC SHOP DETAILS

The unveiling and grand opening for the new Hatter's Toy Shop and Hatter's Music Shop were a huge success. The fairy dressmakers thanked the toy and music shop owners, as all the fairies in the village were asking them to make hats shaped like the new shops. The dressmakers knew these unusual hats would be wonderful for the fairies, their children, parades, celebrations, and everything fun and jovial.

Piano

Trumpet

Drum

Harp

Some instruments are fashioned from delicate flowers, but that's usually only for special occasions.

Bass Horn

Shopkeeper's ladder

Musical Instruments

Secret entrance

MUSICAL INSTRUMENTS

Music is a favorite pastime in the forest. Many great singers and musicians bring about the sweetest spirit and feelings of wonderful contentment with their music. One of the special things about Fairy Village instruments is that they are designed to mimic the sounds of birds, babbling brooks, and rustling winds.

Tenor Horn

Horn

Trumpet

Harp

Bass Horn

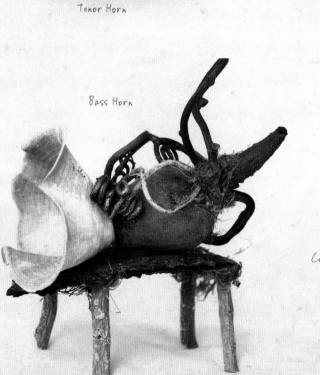

Cello

Violin

Music Stand

THE FAIRY SEAMSTRESS SHOP

A tiny fairy mannequin.

One of the most talented and particular seamstress fairies, who had been sewing with her tiny needle and colorful thread for a very long time, wanted to have her own little seamstress shop. She inquired of her friend, the forest elf named Thomin, to see if he might be able to build her a wonderful shop out of an old hatbox she found in the village of the humans. He agreed happily, and within no time at all, her little shop was finished. And what a joyous and fascinating place it was!

LEFT: The little seamstress fairy worked alongside Thomin to help add thick, beautiful moss to the roof, leaving the sides of the old hatbox exposed.

TOP-RIGHT: Every resourceful fairy seamstress must have an abundance of beautiful fabrics, laces, and velvet flowers on hand in her shop. This dressmaker can run down the stairs to an adorable little cubby to search out her needed treasures, so perfectly close at hand.

All around the fairy lay pretty scraps of fabrics, laces, velvets, and trims needed for her enchanting creations. What inspiration surrounds this talented little artist!

As the busy dressmaker sat at her sewing machine, singing while she worked, many forest friends would visit her. The butterflies (sometimes called "flutterbys"), dragonflies, bees, and other flying creatures would gently float into her shop, as the entire front of her little dwelling was open to the fresh air and sunshine. Sometimes, to her happy delight, she would even receive a surprise visit from tiny ladybugs who would enter through the lovely open windows behind her, quietly landing on her shoulder as she worked.

As the busy little dressmaker always has many gowns and dresses to make for the pretty fairies of the forest, she needs all of her materials and tools close at hand. If she needs more colorful thread or ribbons for a particular gown, she can just run up the stairs near her work table and gather up what she lacks.

One afternoon, when the fairy seamstress was taking a much-needed walk in the woods after a busy week of sewing, she came across an abandoned little cottage. Inside she discovered packages of sewing patterns that must have been left just for her! The salvager that she was, she gathered them up and used them to cover the floors and walls of her busy little shop.

SEWING MACHINE

This enchanting little sewing machine was made by a very creative elf, a dear friend of the fairy seamstress. He found the black root that makes up the heavier part of the machine while walking by the sea one day and later gathered tiny tendrils and pieces of bark to finish the piece. The little fairy was utterly delighted when her friend brought this amazing object for her to use in her magical shop!

The seamstress's most cherished work is beading. She sits by her window, listening to the sweet stories of little bees and dragonflies as she sews each bead onto a lovely piece of fabric, smiling at the comical tales told by her tiny friends.

CHAIR & WORKTABLE

Even the fairy's little chair and worktable are stitched with great care and artistry. She loves showing beauty in everything she makes.

Her tiny pincushions are quite amusing, made from little pods and stuffing. She is a very resourceful seamstress.

MATERIALS

Boxes of tiny buttons, velvet flowers, threads, and beaded fabrics are always close by for the little designer to use. She is well known for her wondrous ability to embellish her lovely gowns with a magical aura of beauty.

FAIRY DRESS SHOP

Fairies are known to be the most wonderful seamstresses. With tiny, meticulous stitches, they create the most beautiful, delicate dresses, hats, and crowns—even little shoes and purses. Together they built this lovely Fairy Dress Shop with its pretty flowered roof to display their wonderful creations. You can visit their shop any day and find them busy sewing new designs to delight you.

LEFT: Pink is one of the fairies' most favorite colors, but pink and white together make a fairy's dream come true. With a lovely pink velvet bodice and delicate sleeves of sheer material, tied with that rare lavender fabric with tiny gold flecks, this dress is greatly admired by all. The fairies love the tiny pink velvet flowers on the shoulders and the pretty pink beaded necklace on this elegant gown; they are amazed at the little seamstress's wonderful talent as a designer.

Fairies are quite resourceful, making their pretty shop sign from tiny curled tendrils. They've even devised a curious way of creating paint from flowers.

Sometimes large crowds of fairies from neighboring villages wait patiently to view the little seamstress's amazing new designs. The busy dressmakers open the entire front wall of their shop, like a huge door, to reveal their newest creations to the anxiously waiting crowd.

This pretty Fairy Dress Shop was a dream come true. The fairies designed and sewed for many months to finally display their tiny dresses and hats for all to see.

Inside the flowered dress shop, the visitor will discover intricate, lovely dresses, all ready to wear to an enchanted dance. The fairies found tiny bits of delicate fabric they used for their pretty dresses in an old abandoned castle. There were even little spools of thread and velvet flowers. Who had left these wonderful treasures?

HATS

For months, the little seamstresses also work together to think of new styles for their hats; they know every fairy will want a lovely new hat to wear to the next spring celebration.

Fairies often have quite a cute sense of humor, and this charming pink crown certainly shows the quirky side of their personalities.

One of the little fairy seamstresses knows just what she wants to make—a large brimmed hat with tiny silver sequins and yellow golden flower trim. She sets about creating the vision she had in her mind, and soon, her beautiful hat is ready to share with her seamstress friends.

Fairy Garden Gazebo

In the lovely spring and summer months, the forest and meadows are filled with beautiful flowers, wild herbs, and grasses. The fairies and their friends love to gather as many blooming plants as they can to make pretty bouquets for all their houses. Early afternoons are often spent in the enchanting garden of the meadow where the fairy gazebo invites all to dream within its magical glass walls. No one knows who built the Fairy Garden Gazebo. There was an old legend, however, of a quiet hobbit who was said to have carved the beautiful glass house from stone and ice.

The most beautiful part of the Fairy Garden Gazebo is the lovely carved stone bird perched at the very top of the bower, whose soft spirit seemed to watch over everyone who entered the glistening door.

LEFT: Inside the rustic retreat, the fairies, elves, and sprites would bring their favorite chairs and table to sit and enjoy the warm sun shimmering through the ice-glass walls. Their furnishings were elegant and gave a wonderful contrast to the natural appearance of the gazebo.

Evenings find poet fairies and storytelling elves under lovely candlelight, the glow reflecting onto the shimmering chandelier above.

The door to the garden gazebo has an unusual design in the middle, also carved from stone. Like a crest or sheaves of wheat, everyone wondered what the old hobbit meant by including this mysterious shape. It adds something curious and wonderful to the beautiful bower.

THE SEA SHELL SHOP

One day, a curious fairy moved into the Fairy Village. She had come many miles from the coast and the home and shop she built was very different from those of the fairies from the forest. Little stairs led up to a shelf filled with shells and a curious stand of books. A glimmering beaded chandelier gracefully dangled above other objects from the sea. A chair, table, and other intricate shells were placed in another corner of the room. The other fairies of the village love to browse her collection of exotic shells.

The fairy's collection includes snail shells, limpets, conches, whelks, cockles, and more treasures of the sea.

An amazing, tiny painting of a ship at sea seemed to sway along the wall, as if it were floating past her.

LEFT: Can you imagine, if you were very small, what it would be like to walk up these amazing stairs and discover this beautiful collection of shells? Someone has also left these little books about the world of the sea. Would you take them home with you to read and ponder upon their curious arrival?

THE PAVILION

airies, elves, gnomes, and hobbits love nothing better than a quiet evening under the Pavilion with the setting sun warming the soft air. Flowers surround the Pavilion with their delicate fragrance. Fairy bakers often fill the table with leftover delicacies, and all the fairies gather together to await the evening dance.

After a long day's work, the Pavilion is the perfect place for hardworking elves and gnomes to relax and visit with their fairy friends.

LEFT: A teapot fashioned from pods and tendrils is a fitting vessel for elf favorites like elderberry tea and twilight nectar.

BELOW: The forest spread is always bounteous: apples, berries, ripe cheese, fresh bread from the village bakery, elderberry tea, and more grace the long community table.

The intricate construction of the Pavilion shows elf and fairy handicraft at its finest.

Cottages

As quirky and delightful as the fairies that occupy them, the cottages in the Fairy Village are wonderfully unique in personality and design. Here we'll showcase some of the most unusual homes we saw during our visit to the village.

THE ARTIST'S COTTAGE

This charming little cottage with its imaginative, angular shape is the home of the village artist elf and his wife, who both love to paint. Their little home keeps them warm and cozy with the moss walls and thick driftwood.

This wonderful little home surely must be filled with cheer every day with such a brightly colored window of pretty yellow flower petals, like the sunshine itself.

The elf artist loves to draw and paint. His wife surprised him one day by framing all of his lovely paintings and displaying them on the walls. The framed paintings brighten their day with happy color and charm.

The little blue embroidered chair looks so cozy next to the table, all fitted out with teacups and a bowl of blueberries. What a happy little home.

Artwork adorns nearly every inch of this little cottage. The painting below is a beautiful rendition of the famous Fairy Castle.

Perhaps they love to read too, as a charming book rests on the table with a lamp that is perfect for reading their favorite story late into the night.

THE FAIRY'S COTTAGE

This rustic cottage looks as though it has been here for hundreds of years, covered with thick, green moss, windblown and tossed as if it were perched atop a mountain by the sea. Weathered and full of old charm, surely someone special lives in this little dwelling.

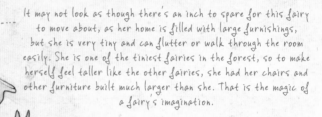

It may not look as though there's an inch to spare for this fairy to move about, as her home is filled with large furnishings, but she is very tiny and can flutter or walk through the room easily. She is one of the tiniest fairies in the forest, so to make herself feel taller like the other fairies, she had her chairs and other furniture built much larger than she. That is the magic of a fairy's imagination.

Foxes are intelligent, loyal, and make wonderful friends!

BELOW: Inside this little forest home, one can see a delightful setting for a talented fairy who looks as though they love to sew and decorate. Two tiny chairs embellished with leaf lace, soft green velvet cushions, moss, and tiny pods sit comfortably next to a tiny, elegant table.

No one knows who first built the Deep Woods Cottage, but it has been a treasured hideaway for village fairies for centuries.

THE DEEP WOODS COTTAGE

Set in a spectacular clearing deep in the woods, this cottage is an unusual dwelling with its two floors, glass windows, and a wraparound porch where fairies love to listen to the brook and morning birdsong. Fairies and elves use the Deep Woods Cottage as a retreat from the bustle of the Fairy Village.

The cottage's magnificent woodland setting is echoed in the fine woodworking throughout the dwelling.

This little balcony is a favorite spot to watch as the early morning sun turns the sleepy forest a cheerful gold.

Skilled dwarves must have done the challenging work of creating the round and square windows.

The cottage roofs were beautifully tiled with cedar wood from deep in the forest.

THE THREE SISTERS

he Three Sisters is a wonderful trio of beautiful cottages. They serve as an inn for traveling fairy folk visiting the village from far off lands. The cottages were built by three fairy sisters who were known far and wide for their kindness and bounteous hospitality.

The Three Sisters

Guestroom 1 with music suite

Guestroom 3

Guestroom 2

Community activities room

Lending library

Sitting room

THE FAIRY TREEHOUSE

The Fairy Treehouse and Fairy Castle were built many years ago. The Fairy Treehouse was begun first. It started as just one little house, but over many generations, it grew to be a large dwelling of many rooms, stairways, balconies, hidden alcoves, and gardens with an amazing observatory at the very top. Since then, several of the younger fairies flew off into the forest and some of the elves, gnomes, and hobbits trundled away to other lands. But there were still so many little people living in the Fairy Treehouse that they needed more room. Those who remained began creating the Fairy Castle and Fairy Village.

GARDEN ROOM

GUEST READING ROOM

From ancient pianos to charming windowboxes, tiny delights wait around every corner in the Fairy Treehouse.

GRAND STAIRCASE

DINING ROOM

OBSERVATORY

ALCOVE GUEST ROOM

TREEHOUSE ROOMS (SOUTH SIDE)

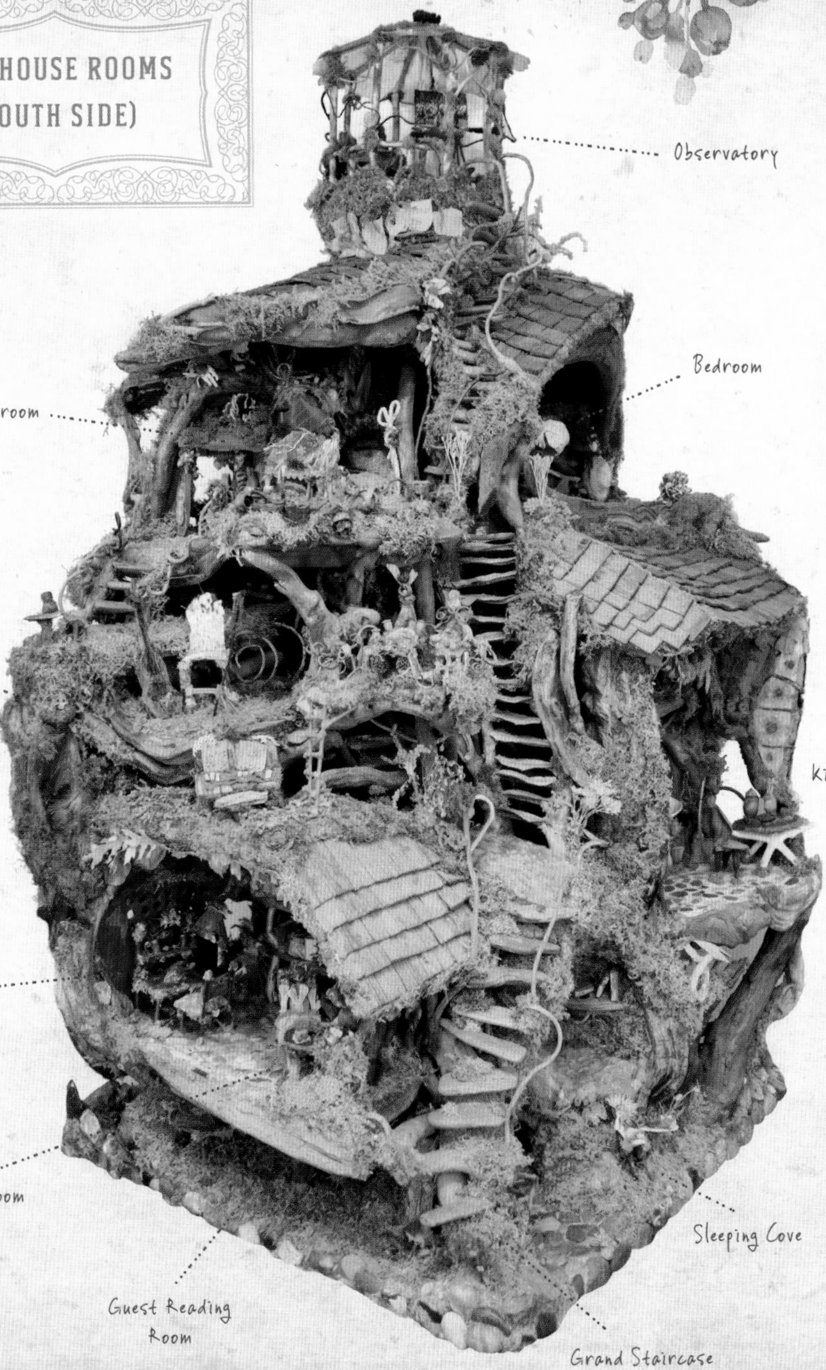

Observatory
Bedroom
Upper Bedroom
Music Balcony
Kitchen
Library
Music Room
Sleeping Cove
Guest Reading Room
Grand Staircase

MUSIC ROOM

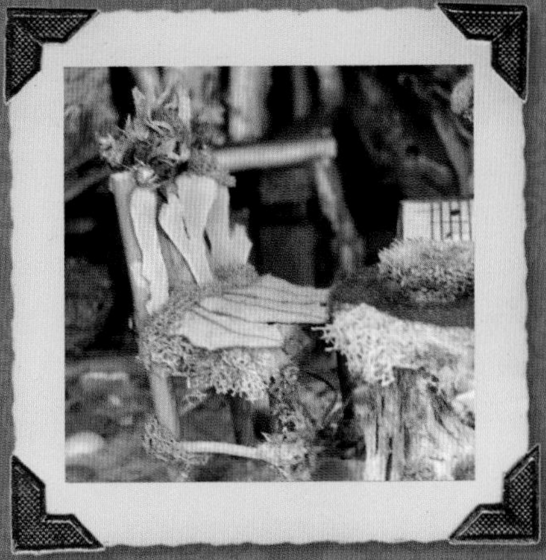

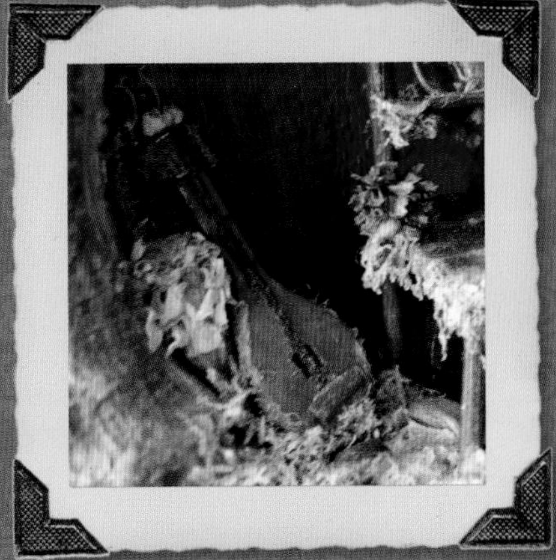

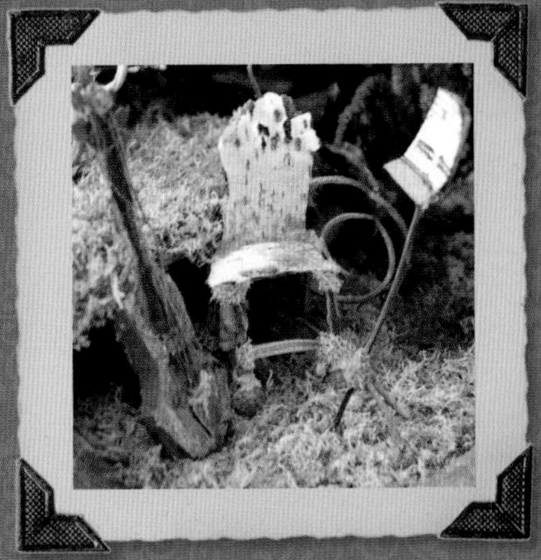

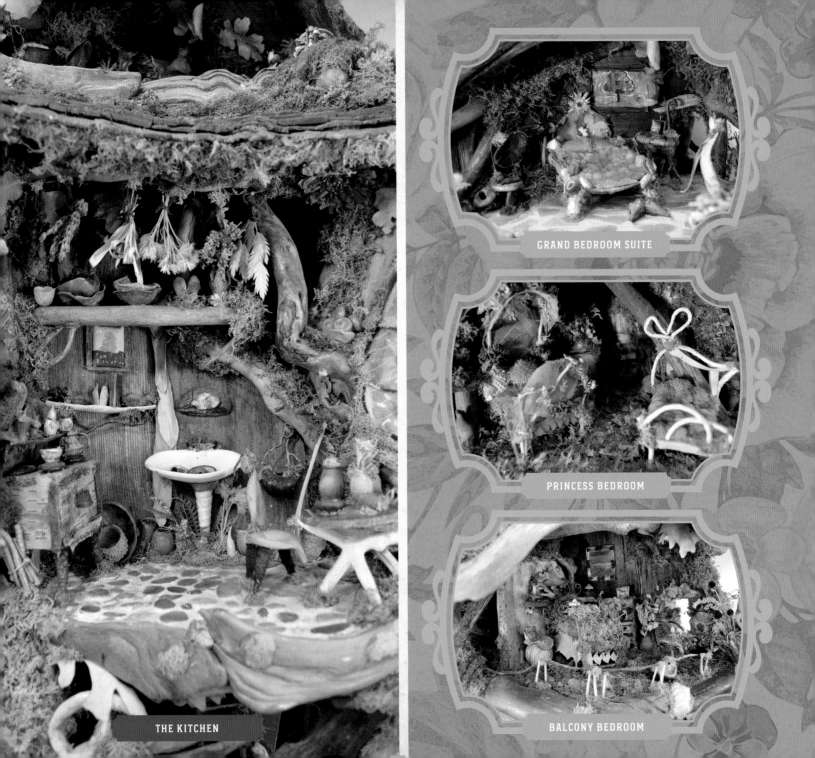

THE KITCHEN

GRAND BEDROOM SUITE

PRINCESS BEDROOM

BALCONY BEDROOM

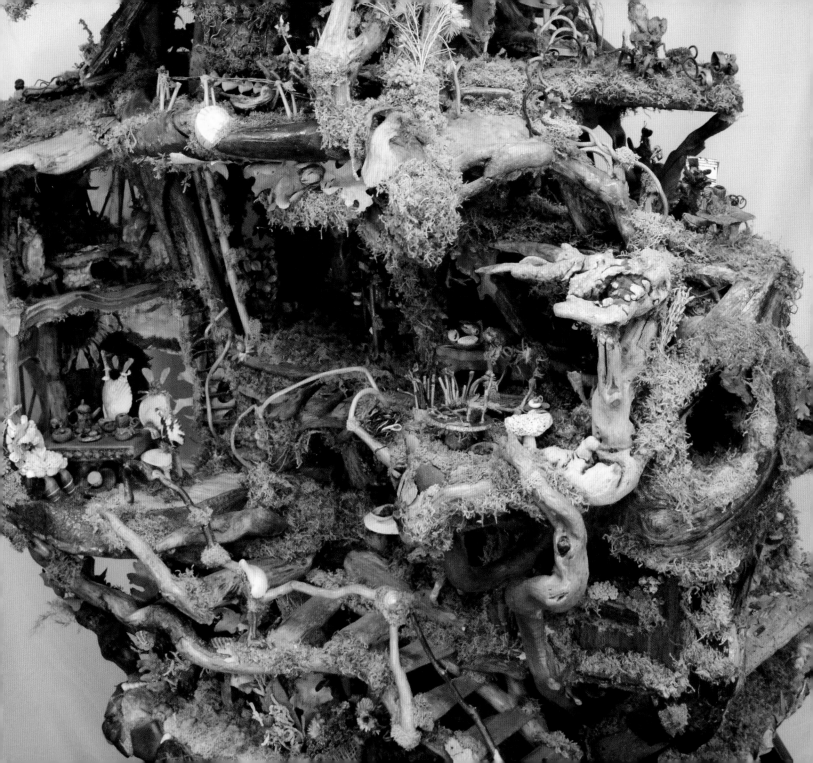

Pussy willows make a
wonderfully soft bed in the
sleeping cove tucked under
the stairs.

Though the fairies do source some furniture pieces from the village, they also enjoy making some in their beautiful fairy house.

THE FAIRY CASTLE

airyland is a magical land, and the fairy homes are wonderful, enchanted dwellings. Fairy houses are not easy for humans to find because they blend in with the trees, but they also have special guardians who protect all of the forest homes. Fairies like to hide their cottages in the hills and under trees, but wherever they are, they always keep their eyes on the village below. The most important of these homes is the Fairy Castle, which has long been a place of safety and joy for the fairies of Fairy Village in even the worst of times. It is also the summer residence of the Fairy Queen herself.

The Fairy Queen is the guardian of all woodland fairies, elves, hobbits, and gnomes.

The Fairy Castle is filled with the finest art, furniture, and embellishments the fairy craftsmen could create.

LEFT: The Fairy Castle's most iconic features are its three soaring towers. One houses an observatory, another an art studio, and the third serves as a quiet hermitage for the most studious fairies and elves. Fairies usually build smaller structures that are easier to hide, but the towers on the Fairy Castle serve as important lookout points for the entire village.

Many of the castle's features were patterned from ancient castles in the fairies homeland.

THE HERMITAGE

BEDROOM

POWDER ROOM

READING CORNER

CASTLE (NORTH SIDE)

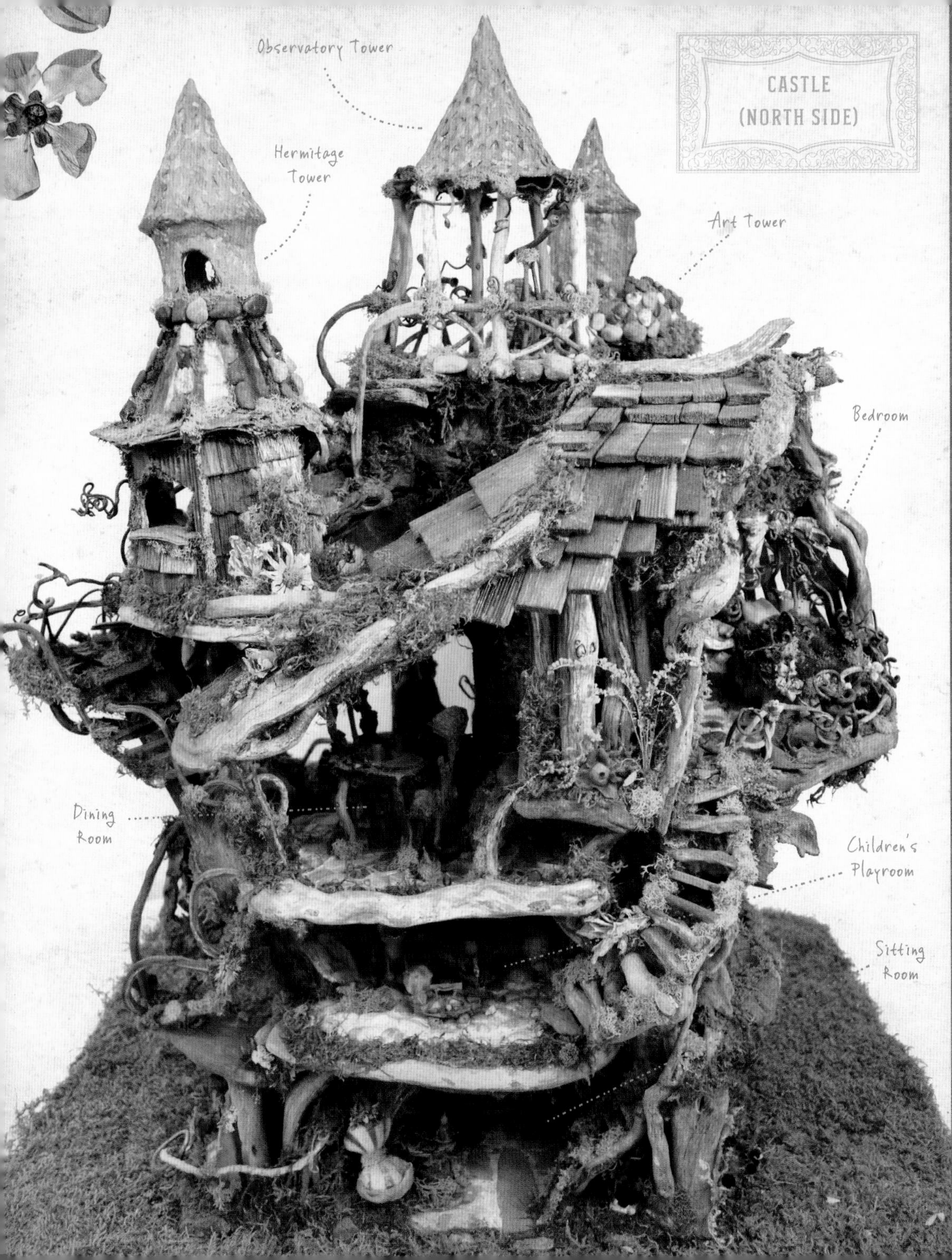

Observatory Tower
Hermitage Tower
Art Tower
Bedroom
Dining Room
Children's Playroom
Sitting Room

ART TOWER STUDIOS

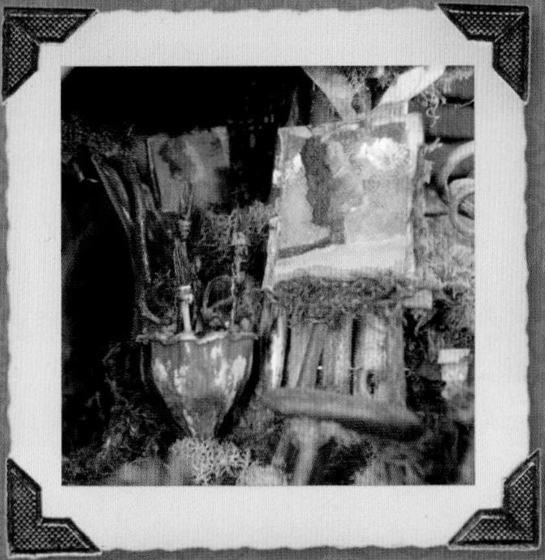

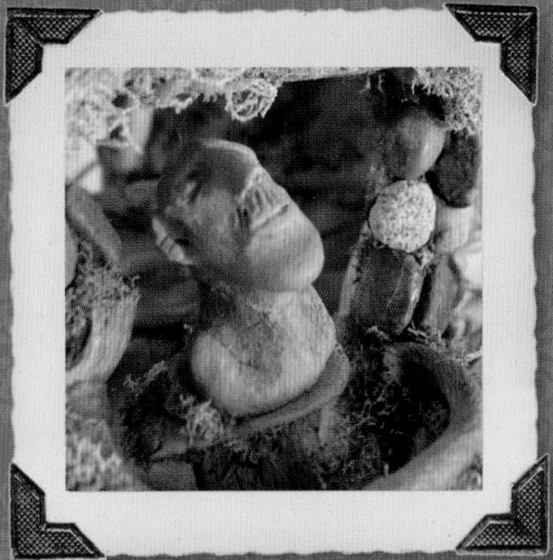

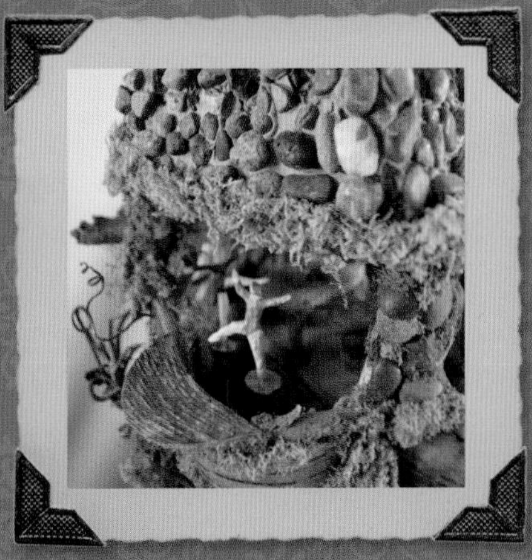

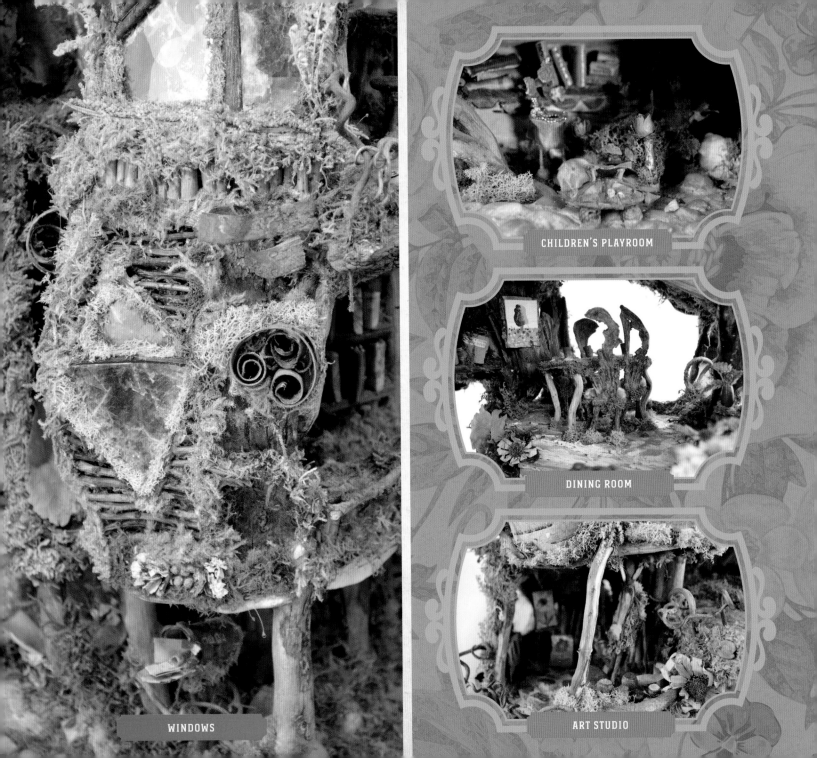

WINDOWS

CHILDREN'S PLAYROOM

DINING ROOM

ART STUDIO

The Fairy Castle requires fulltime laundry service to keep its residents and guests comfortable at all times.

Acknowledgments

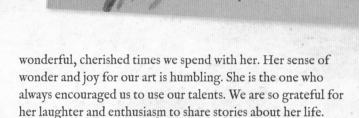

We first want to express our gratitude to Familius. We couldn't find a more perfect group of people to work with to represent our creativity and to honor for their sincere love of families.

A very special thank you to Christopher Robbins, our wonderful publisher, for his kindness and incredible belief in our art. His cheerful, positive example is inspiring, and his vision to bring uplifting books to the world is truly worth believing in.

We want to give our heartfelt appreciation to David Miles, our book designer, for his endless optimism and patience. His collaborative spirit helped us find the most creative ideas to make *Fairy Village* possible. Thank you, David, for presenting our art in such a beautiful setting and for bringing your own sensitive artistry to make this a truly extraordinary book.

We give special gratitude to Brooke Jorden for overseeing *Fairy Village*, for keeping us on schedule, and for seeing that it all came together. We appreciate her cheerful guidance.

A very grateful thank you to Laurie Duersch, who edited what we labored over with what seemed like a gentle breeze. Her wonderful skills brought us a new appreciation for writing.

Thank you to Sarah Echard for her work as copyeditor and for using her professionalism to make *Fairy Village* more enjoyable for our readers.

A special thank you to Ashley Mireles for being so cheerful and prompt in filling our requests for more copies of our books.

Our deepest gratitude to Barbara Poulshock, Debbie's amazing mother, for her cheerful outlook on life and the wonderful, cherished times we spend with her. Her sense of wonder and joy for our art is humbling. She is the one who always encouraged us to use our talents. We are so grateful for her laughter and enthusiasm to share stories about her life.

We want to express our gratitude for our wonderful sons, Michael and Matthew, for the happiness they bring us and the

blessing they are to us every day. We cherish and admire them for their faith, their optimism, their hard work, and the love they have for their families.

We are very thankful to Caressa and Brittnee, our daughters-in-law, for their wonderful examples and the encouragement and support they give our sons, whose lives are abundantly happier because of them. We've grown to appreciate them both more and more every day.

We thank our three precious granddaughters—Aunika, Lilly, and Nova—whose amazing smiles, laughter, and energy give us such happiness; we've become younger and more grateful for life because of them. We cherish every moment with them and listen to their every word with wondrous delight.

We express our thanks to our brothers and Mike's sisters for their kindness, their encouraging support over the years, their wonderful examples of hard work and faith, and their great sense of humor.

Thank you to our dearest friends, Rick and Derlene Housley and their family, for their precious friendship and the wonderful experiences we've had together over all these years. As they've said, "It takes a long time to grow a friend."

A heartfelt thank you to Missy and Dan Barker for their wonderful friendship, for being the best of all neighbors, and for bringing us so many amazing antiques and vintage finds.

Thank you to JoAnne Webster for her kindred spirit and friendship and for the special props she contributed for our book. We have so enjoyed getting to know her.

Thank you to Cate Gable, whose kindness and enjoyment of our art was truly appreciated. We were so grateful to have our little shop, if even for a short time, thanks to her.

Thank you to the many people who visited our shop, Fairy House Vintage, in Ocean Park, Washington, while we wrote our book and for their cheerful encouragement. We are grateful for the wonderful welcome we were given by this gem of a community.

About the Authors

Debbie and Mike exhibiting The Fairy Castle in Brooklyn, New York.

DEBBIE SCHRAMER

Working on our second book, *Fairy Village*, has given me such a wonderful sense of fulfillment and more faith in myself. To share my talents with so many people is very humbling but also an exciting realization for me, as I have been creative for most of my life. I began writing poetry at age eleven, wanting to express my love for my family and the beauty of life. I still remember my parents' emotional response to my first attempts at sharing my thoughts on paper through poetry. I had no idea something I would write could mean so much to someone else. I began to believe in my capabilities, unable to draw upon them before. I continue to write poetry, sharing the thoughts and dreams I hold close to my heart. That first poem held a bright light for me that has never dimmed.

I have learned through writing our books that I can reach out to the world more easily now. I have always envisioned helping people, through my talents, to see the beauty in the world and in others, because there is nobility and inherent goodness in people and in life that is important to remember. Through my art, I have been able to show the beauty of the earth; through my poetry and children's stories, I have shared the beauty of the human spirit and how kindness can heal one another.

Perhaps the most important thought I would like to share in this book is to believe in oneself. Whatever form of creativity one chooses to follow, it is a wonderful gift to accept the talents you have and develop them with all the faith and gratitude you hold. I am grateful for the realization I had years ago when I first began to paint that I didn't need to compare my artistic abilities to those of others. My style and talent are different from other artists but still unique in their own way, which is what art is about. When I learned to appreciate my own artistic style, I was finally able to enjoy my paintings or whatever medium I was working in. That knowledge has truly helped me to love being an artist and grow in my talents. It is important to me to share that awareness with others, to help them believe in themselves and their wonderful natural abilities.

I come from a very creative family of artists, writers, musicians, opera singers, and teachers. My childhood was very happy, filled with the enthusiasm and energy of creative people. It was their love of the arts and of expression that motivated me to look for the talents that I, too, might possess. I am very grateful to have grown up in such an amazing, imaginative family.

My father was a wonderful jazz pianist, violist, composer, and teacher; he was a very gentle, kind man. My mother sang and taught opera, and now at ninety years old (though retired) is still a classical pianist and a composer and directs choirs and musical drama groups. Memories of my childhood are filled with movie-like scenes of my mother singing beautiful, dramatic songs in German or French and my father at the piano playing his Erroll Garner style of music in impromptu jam sessions as we would all dance around the living room. There was always a myriad of fascinating friends and relatives dropping over to talk, play music, and just cherish the excitement of life. I remember my parents visiting with their musician friends at our house; their excitement and laughter was fascinating to me as I sat in a corner across the room listening to their humorous and excited conversations. It was that energy and love of life that gave me an appreciation for

Mike and Debbie

people and their unique personalities and talents. I loved our life as a family; it was truly different and wonderful.

My brothers are very artistic as well. My older brother, David, is very appreciative of the arts, working as a screenwriter, filmmaker, and jazz pianist. My younger brother, Joe, is an English teacher in Japan and a musician and composer with an incredible sense of humor. My grandfather was a musician in Hollywood for the Dave Rose Orchestra, who played for Bing Crosby, Red Skelton, Phil Harris, and others. My aunt was a wonderful painter. I am also related to Ralph Waldo Emerson, which was very exciting to learn because I am a writer too. It's wonderful to be part of such a creative family.

I am originally from Los Angeles, born in August of 1950, but grew up in Garden Grove and Surfside, California. As I reflect fondly upon my childhood years, I am reminded of the lovely environment my brothers and I grew up in. Our home was always filled with beautiful antiques, musical instruments, and my mother's artistic flair for decorating. There was such a happy atmosphere; I felt a great sense of comfort and freedom to be myself. In Garden Grove, we lived in a large, old home with a beautiful, expansive yard. We had many old avocado trees, a fish pond, and a large barn. My most vivid memories are of running through the yard with the canopy of trees above me and hydrangea flowers and other lush plants surrounding the grayish-blue two-story house. I have always been happiest when I am outside, especially when I was young; that was complete freedom for me.

My parents' little bungalow home in Surfside was right across from the ocean; the beach was our front yard. My brothers and I would spend hours outside running through the sand and just feeling the beauty of the sea, the fresh air, and the wondrous expanse of space.

We later moved to Klamath Falls, Oregon, the summer before I started fourth grade. My parents bought an older hunter's cabin high up on a hill overlooking a beautiful wildlife refuge of marshes and creeks filled with amazing birds and animals. As a young person, I was terrified of living in such an isolated place at first, but it wasn't long before my fears fell away and I began to cherish the woods and mountains around us. I spent many hours by myself walking through the forest and trails around our home. The time I spent alone in nature at this time in my life truly influenced my love of the outdoor world. I think it was this experience of living in the beautiful forest, with its expansive views of quiet marshes, the sounds of the birds, and the scent of the deer lilies in the summer, that really inspired me to cherish nature as I do. I wasn't afraid but instead found a wonderful peace and contentment as I felt the spirits of the trees, the sky, the birds, and the air. The wonderful influence of nature gave me a very deep love for the gentle spirit of life. I felt that this was my home in a way, like a kindred spirit world on earth.

My poetry was often filled with my deep appreciation for nature, and I was also inspired by children, art, literature, and the expressive faces of people—their loneliness and joy, their dreams and ideas. But I was especially moved to write from my yearnings to know God. I felt closest to his spirit when I was out in nature.

I began writing children's stories in the early 1980s when our two sons, Michael and Matthew, were just toddlers; I was very inspired by them and found such great delight and happiness in being a mother. Their enthusiasm for life and ability to find joy in everything was amazing to me. Michael became a composer, and Matthew, a filmmaker; they now have wonderful wives and families of their own with three daughters between them. Our granddaughters have brought us such a wonderful, renewed joy for life, as our sons still do. Their sweet spirits help us feel like children again, encouraging us to see life with new eyes and hearts.

My husband and I began creating our nature art in 1987 while living in Washington on a little farm next to my parents. We always enjoyed gathering wildflowers and grasses on our long walks. We grew large vegetable and flower gardens and built a greenhouse and barn for the growing menagerie of animals we had been gathering. As winter approached, we could feel our happiness begin to dim, as we knew we would have to wait until spring to work outside in our gardens again. So we brought many of our flowers, herbs, wild grasses, and other natural treasures into our workroom to dry, not yet knowing how we would use them. Earlier, I had attempted to build a life-size Adirondack-style chair using large branches from our yard, but it didn't withstand actual use, so I was prompted to follow Mike's suggestion of making a miniature twig chair. Creating my first small piece from branches, flowers, and moss was very exciting! I was so happy with my first little chair that I made several other pieces. Working with natural materials was inspiring and calming for me. When Mike arrived home from work, he was quite surprised to see my menagerie of little furniture, so he began creating wonderful fairytale pieces as well.

We began participating in different art shows and festivals and exhibiting our pieces at boutiques and libraries. Then in February of 1991, our fairy furniture was featured in a beautiful article in *Victoria* magazine. We were astonished to receive over eight hundred letters from their readers, who loved our small fairy works of art. We created our first catalog, chose the business name Whimsical Twigs, and have been creating our nature art ever since.

From that day on, our house became a fanciful home of little, magical furnishings for fairies, elves, and gnomes. We added tiny tables, beds, shelves, cradles, armoires, lamps, dishes, books, and everything from a home you can imagine,

all made from the world of nature. We also began creating small houses as well, and in 1993, we made our first large fairy house, which we called the Fairy Treehouse. It was exhibited at the Folklife Festival in Seattle, Washington, and was received with such an amazing response from everyone. In 1995, after a phenomenal response to our nature art by Rebecca Hoffberger, the founder and director of the American Visionary Art Museum in Baltimore, Maryland, our Fairy Treehouse was shown in their inaugural exhibit entitled *The Tree of Life*. Many of our small fairy furniture pieces were also included in the museum. Our mossy fairy home was truly enjoyed by all visitors; it was chosen as the fourth-favorite work of art from the exhibit's four hundred pieces, so we were very touched by this incredible response.

In 2012, the American Visionary Art Museum again included our nature art in another year-long exhibit called *The Art of Storytelling*. The Fairy Treehouse and a new house we created, the Fairy Castle, were shown in a stunning display designed by Rebecca Hoffberger along with many of our fairy furniture pieces. We were very humbled by such incredible appreciation of our art and the love that people showed for our creations.

As our art career continued to blossom, we developed a video catalog, a card line, more elaborate and unique pieces for fairies and other forest people, larger fairy houses, and other natural sculptural works. Our art pieces have been featured in many books and magazines and sold in many shops, galleries, and museums all over the United States and several other countries. Private collectors and other artists have enjoyed our work as well. Our nature art has given us many exciting opportunities that have truly touched our hearts as artists and as people; our faith in our abilities and talents has grown so much. We know these are not of our own making but are given from our creator. We are very grateful to share these wonderful gifts with others.

Along with creating our own art, we have also taught children's art classes, helping them learn how to make art from the beautiful world of nature, which has been a very heartwarming experience. Children are amazing natural artists.

They have a way of expressing themselves in any kind of art form that is very joyful and spontaneous. We are always amazed at the way children approach art and what their creations mean to them. Their sense of humor and perspective about art is bright and imaginative, bringing new inspiration to us every time we work with them.

We began working in other mediums in 1994—painting in acrylic and oils, sculpting with driftwood and papier-mâché, and collage and assemblage with paper and found objects. In 2000, Mike started doing sculptures in bronze; his work was amazing and brought out yet another of his incredible talents. In 2007, we worked with our sons on making our first film, *The Enchanted Treehouse*, a charming movie about our nature art. It was a wonderful experience to share our talents as a family; it was also exciting to combine our art in a film with storytelling, music, stop-motion animation, puppetry, and voiceover. We look forward to making more films in the future, as it is such a great medium for different kinds of talents. Our confidence as artists has grown immensely with the success of our nature art. Creating in other mediums expanded our love of being artists and gave us more ways to express ourselves.

In 2012, we had the opportunity to work with disabled adults in daily art classes for painting, sculpture, collage, and other mediums. It was amazing to see how art gave them a calmer spirit and more confidence in their abilities. Those who could be very unpredictable and temperamental became more soft spoken and cooperative. The students who were shy and more uncommunicative were able to show excitement about their paintings and drawings. We created a website to feature their art and also held several art shows to offer their finished works to the public, which was quite exciting for the students. It was an exceptionally special experience for us; although challenging at times, we were grateful to share our artistic skills with our students.

In 2014, we began collecting and selling antiques and vintage objects. We had always loved beautiful old furniture, books, china, and other lovely pieces, and I had grown up with the wonderful antiques my mother collected. We appreciate the incredible workmanship and history of old things and

Debbie and Mike's brand new museum: Fairy House Vintage and Museum.

enjoy including them along with our art. In 2016, we opened a charming little shop in Ocean Park, Washington, with antiques, vintage, and art. This book, *Fairy Village*, was written in this lovely little town by the sea.

In May of 2017, a dream we have had for many years to own a nature art museum finally came true. We now have a wonderful shop with our antique and vintage treasures along with a museum devoted to our art made from nature. All the wonderful pieces that are included in this book are on display in our new museum, Fairy House Vintage and Museum.

It has been an amazing experience to be an artist; I cannot imagine any other kind of life, as it brings me so much happiness. It is the natural way for me to express my ideas and feelings. Mike and I have found great healing, comfort, and happiness through our art; our expressions of creativity have lifted us to a more beautiful and fascinating place. We, in turn, acknowledge the beauty and joy we experience in our lives as a wonderful gift from God.

We are grateful to be artists so that we can share our joy of life with others and impart beauty and gentleness in the world. We feel that we all need to hear that quiet, still voice within us and look at life as a little child. ☙

I was born in the Fox River Valley in Batavia, Illinois (about thirty miles west of Chicago), on a winter's day in January 1950 in a little house my father built with his two brothers. The story my mother passed down to me was that on Christmas Eve, two weeks before I was to come into the world, my grandmother had invited our family over to visit. My dad had replied that my mother wasn't feeling well, so my grandmother suggested he turn the television on for her and then he could come over with my three older brothers. The classic movie *A Christmas Carol* was playing; the entire evening, my mother was unable to get up and change the channel. I think she felt a bit jilted by the experience and never liked watching that timeless story ever again.

My grandmother's house was just around the corner from my parents' house. One could walk through the open, unfenced backyards of our relatives to get to their house. My grandmother's grandfather was an Irishman from Londonderry and the first carpenter to settle in Batavia with the first scouting party. He purchased a large tract of land just west of the Fox River, which became known as the Irish patch. As family members married, they were given a bit a land to build a house. That is how my grandmother received her land, house, and the two lots my dad and his brother built their houses on.

My mother's father's family were all Irish and lived next door to her as she grew up in St. Charles. Her aunts used to call me "the little leprechaun." There ended up being nine children given to my parents to raise, so I was never without the company of youthful personalities, cute faces, or happy children as I was growing up.

My parents grew up in religious families, both having aunts and uncles who were nuns and priests. My mother learned her prayers in Gaelic. You might say I had a proper Catholic upbringing with pictures of saints adorning my room, little prayer books to read, and endless feast days and devotions.

Many hours of my childhood were spent staring up at the religious statues in our church and school, pondering, praying, and studying the lines and forms of the figures. My older brother Jim and my mother first taught me to love books, and my older brother Steve taught me to carve faces on little pieces of wood with a pocket knife. It was an interesting life, growing up under my older brothers; they raised homing pigeons and rabbits, built medieval lances for jousting, fashioned multicolored, hand-painted shields out of old wood, and made medieval clothing and helmets. We were always playing make-believe.

When they were at school and I was still home, I would often go out to the garage to look at my dad's tools. They resided in a very old metal toolbox, which he had made while working in the shipyards in Charleston, South Carolina, during World War II. I was fascinated by the tools and was quite content to just look at them and imagine where they had been and how they had been used. Later, my dad taught me how to saw and hammer but grew frustrated with my left-handedness and sent me into the house to help my mother. I felt I was doomed to domestic work. I lamented seeing my brothers continue to learn other skills. My brothers did help me build soapbox derby cars out of old baby buggies and wheels (which we always had a good supply of with nine children in the family). My remorse at not furthering my education of the tools in the garage may have planted the seed for our present work, as now I am building what I felt like I never got a chance to build. To this day, I prefer to use hand tools. I do not employ power tools in any of our work because they are noisy and I prefer to work quietly; I use only hammers, saws, knives, and chisels to carve and build everything and make things fit. All of my brothers grew to be very proficient in building. I, on the other hand, was left to use my imagination, and that is how I have lived my life—with my head half in the clouds.

My father had great sayings, such as "Michael, use your head for more than a hat rack" or "Money doesn't grow on trees." He also used to say "You can do anything you put your mind to." He was quite a genius in his own way. People used to bring him ideas they had for inventions, and he would draw up the plans for them so they could get them manufactured. Later in life when he was retired and our little art business was growing, he thought he should visit us to help us to catch up on our orders. I never told him I'd found a way to make a living from things that "grow on trees," but I enjoy the irony.

My father's father was born to German farming immigrants from the area north of Trier. My father's grandfather, my great-grandfather, had a small business building, installing, and repairing windows, doors, and sashes. I think in my DNA I may have some of my great-grandfather's skills. I often feel a connection to people from my past as I sit and work quietly, making our buildings and little furniture. In a picture of my family tree, there are weavers, carpenters, farmers, shoemakers, and who knows what else.

One colorful story my mother would tell was of her father's family who were from Ireland, in the counties of Meath and Westmeath, in a little parish called Kilbeggan. Her father's family grew up there, farming and draying (hauling with a horse and wagon). Their house had a dirt floor, but their barn had a cement floor, so all their neighbors would gather there for dances.

My mother's grandmother, who was from Mullingar, was a very religious woman. It is told she once prayed for her son the whole time he went out to play a baseball game on Sunday. When she was fresh off the boat in New York from Ireland, someone handed her a banana to eat as a gift for her arrival. Having not seen one before, she started to eat the banana without peeling it, at which she remarked, "The Americans are the oddest people. They eat the most bitter-tasting fruit!"

When I was a boy, we used to have large reunions at the park on the Fox River that included both sides of the family. It was fun to see the old men with their suspenders and garters on their sleeves, tables filled with pies, and old women wearing floral dresses, sturdy black shoes, and wire-rimmed spectacles. One of my mother's uncles who came to the reunions was a farmer and crossbred and invented white popcorn. It was always a fun-filled day, ending with two of my great-aunts,

Rose and Esther, doing an Irish jig on the picnic tabletops.

My father barely made it into my mother's family; they were so insistent that she marry an Irishman, and they thought a name like Schramer would not be good for her. But my mother begged that they at least listen to him sing "Danny Boy," which he did so beautifully that they allowed him to marry her. While growing up, my father loved music. He learned to play musical instruments from an old German man in his town so well that it impressed his mother enough to pay for piano lessons. He eventually settled on singing and playing the trumpet. I felt so blessed to listen to him sing to us when I was small.

My mother was such a happy person, always baking and loving her children; she was so supportive and such a good sport to put up with all of us. When I was in sixth, seventh, and eighth grades, I entered art contests, singing talent shows, and speech tournaments. It was she who helped me rehearse, listened to my lines, and kept coaching and encouraging me to do my art. Later in high school, I again turned to art and drama, this time embracing drama more fully, as the debate classes I had participated in were wearing me out. I could no longer debate the pros and cons of our current events. Using my imagination in the written plays and enjoying the costumes and props were so much more satisfying for me.

From an early age, I had always been more comfortable with my head half in the clouds. I have found that art infuses me with life. The element of creating something from minimal tools and materials was then, and still is, very rewarding for me. Working with my hands and mind, using whatever inspirations come to me, gives me a peace and contentment I cannot otherwise find. I also enjoy thoughtful and intellectual talk shows, good historical period dramas, and documentaries.

I appreciate the storytelling that goes on in our daily lives more fully now. While we were writing *Fairy Village*, we had a little shop in Ocean Park, Washington, where we offered our fairy furniture, paintings, and sculptures as well as antiques and vintage objects. The people who visited our shop loved to talk with us and were a real source of interest to me. I found they had the most interesting stories to tell that were so different than mine, but they, in turn, loved hearing our stories. I am so thrilled to now have a shop in Utah with an open door to continue to visit with people as we move forward in the coming years. I am excited to meet many more people, share our artwork with them, and hear their stories.

Debbie and I started creating art together in the third month of our marriage. We had taken a job as caretakers and sitters for a little boy whose father worked in construction. Occasionally he asked me to help him with his work. We were given a little house on his property and a garden to grow whatever we wanted. It was a welcome relief from living in the city. As we worked in the garden, a group of boys came down to see who we were. They were quite a comical little bunch, and we became good friends. It was there that Debbie and I, for some curious reason or another (we never quite figured out why), began to make small houses from wood, pinecones, and twigs. We cut out ducks from cardboard, painted them, and fastened them up on the walls in the little house in the corners of each room and on the hutches. It was there that Debbie showed me the drawings she had done in a college art

class. I liked them. I saw something different in them than what Debbie had intended. She let me work on her drawings to try to develop them.

Our weekly trips to the library provided us with many types of art to look at. Debbie always found the most interesting books. She is still doing that today, adding curious and beautiful bits of art to her blog, *Beautiful Art*. I was curious about gardening and books about building and baking, which I had taken an interest in at that time. But even with all the art forms we looked at together, we kept going back to working with found objects from nature.

One of the things we have always enjoyed doing is telling a story to the other when one of us cannot sleep. Sometimes they are very interesting stories, but we have never written them down, as we would always just fall asleep. Sometimes we would even take turns adding to a story the other began. Debbie had volumes of poetry which we would read together, but she did not take up drawing and painting until after we had poured ourselves into the fairy furniture and fairy houses we made from nature. Debbie's mother was always telling us, "You are both so talented; you should do something with your talents." We have mostly been inspired to do art when we have had a little space away from crowds—a little plot for gardening and room to work and store the things we gather.

We were born just six months apart, but in different seasons; I in the winter and Debbie in the summer. It certainly has given us different perspectives. With all the acknowledgments we made in this book and in our first book, we are very thankful we have helped each other accomplish all the work we set out to do. At some point when we work together, we catch the vision of what the other is trying to do, and from then on, it is a real joy for each of us to work in our own quiet way, adding this, making that, until the project comes together, such as the village for this book.

The Pacific Northwest, Washington and Oregon, has always been our home, even when we are away from it. There is something special about the people there; they are so friendly and talkative, which we both like. They have an acceptance of the weather and make the most of it. I believe they possess

Debbie and Mike's new museum will showcase their incredible collection of fairy furniture, buildings, and vintage art.

some of the most finely tuned ears from listening to the soft and rhythmic patter of the rain on their roofs and windows.

We have truly enjoyed our life together. One year, our son Matthew made a documentary about us entitled *Married to Art*. It was funny to see ourselves as he saw us. He followed us around as we went outside each day to see what natural materials we could find hidden on our lengthy walks. He told us to just go about our day as we would if he were not there. It was really quite a revelation to me about how much we are committed to creating our little worlds with our art. Soon, our older son, Michael, was recruited to compose music for the documentary. All in all, it was a lot of fun and made me think that we should try to share our work more with others. These were the days before social media and our books. I can see now it was all in preparation for what we are doing today.

These days, when I am not making a new addition to the village for our museum, I love to paint oceans and clouds as I watch the ever-changing winds and rain. Sometimes I'll add an old freighter passing in the distance. I still love to see the big boats that come up the Columbia River. Working around the huge ships in the shipyards in Seattle years ago still influences my work. I am forever fascinated with buildings with small crawl spaces and doors and ladders going everywhere to different levels. Another big influence on me and on my art were the days I spent adjusting my ladder in a myriad of trees as I picked apples in eastern Washington for two seasons. It was such an influence on me because I was on a farm, outdoors all day, miles from other people, working alone, and living in a little cabin with a wood stove. I spent a lot of time in the tops of the trees with the clouds, birds, and mountaintops all around me.

Other places and experiences that have influenced me are the Quinault Rain Forest on the Washington and Oregon coasts, sorting salmon on the docks of Seattle, pushing corn into a conveyor belt in Bellingham, and working as a gardener at a retirement homes for nuns. I cannot forget where it all started on that little farm in Parkland, Washington, where we gardened, gathered wild grasses and flowers, built little cabins, and cared for our animals while enjoying raising our two wonderful sons. That is where, one fall day, we took our love of nature indoors and began to build miniature scenes from our imagination while winter transformed our gardens until the new beginning of spring.

We want to thank all of you who have picked up our little book. It is our wish that it will give you some kind of joy, wonder, and peace. I would like to close with a line from one of Debbie's poems: "Little moonbeams grace my heart, filling me with wonderings and unwavering stillness." This thought sums up how it feels to work on our art; a stillness comes over us that is priceless.

CONNECT WITH MIKE AND DEBBIE SCHRAMER

www.sunflowerhouse.etsy.com

www.mycyclesart.etsy.com

www.fairyhousethebook.etsy.com

www.facebook.com/fairyhousethebook

www.enchantedtreehousemovie.com

VISIT THE MUSEUM

Fairy House Vintage and Museum
36 East 400 North
Provo, UT 84606

www.facebook.com/DebbieandMike2

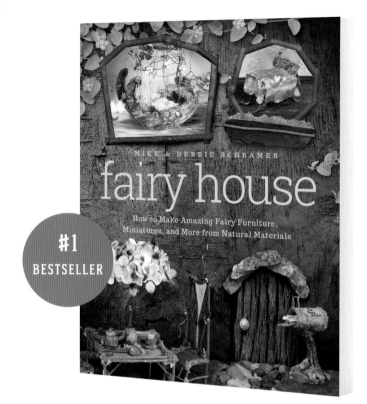

MIKE & DEBBIE SCHRAMER

fairy house

How to Make Amazing Fairy Furniture,
Miniatures, and More from Natural Materials

#1 BESTSELLER

Packed with
hundreds of detailed
photographs.

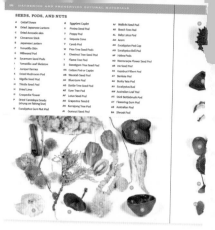

LEARN TO MAKE FAIRY CREATIONS OF YOUR OWN!

Mike and Debbie Schramer share their tips and secrets to creating enchanting works of fairy art in this #1 bestselling instructional guide. *Fairy House* is a fascinating adventure into the making of miniscule kingdoms of the fairytale realm from objects found in nature. Through more than 350 clear, detailed, full-color photographs and understandable yet whimsical guidance, you will learn to fashion an amazing array of beautiful and unique pieces from beautiful beds to tiny teacups to cozy cottages.

ISBN-13: 978-1-939629-69-2

Price: $24.95 (USD)

Specs: Paperback with flaps, 192 pages, 8 x 10

Category: Crafts

Easy, step-by-step
instructions with
photos for every step!

Includes a guide to selecting
and drying natural materials
for craft use.

FAMILIUS

AVAILABLE WHEREVER BOOKS ARE SOLD

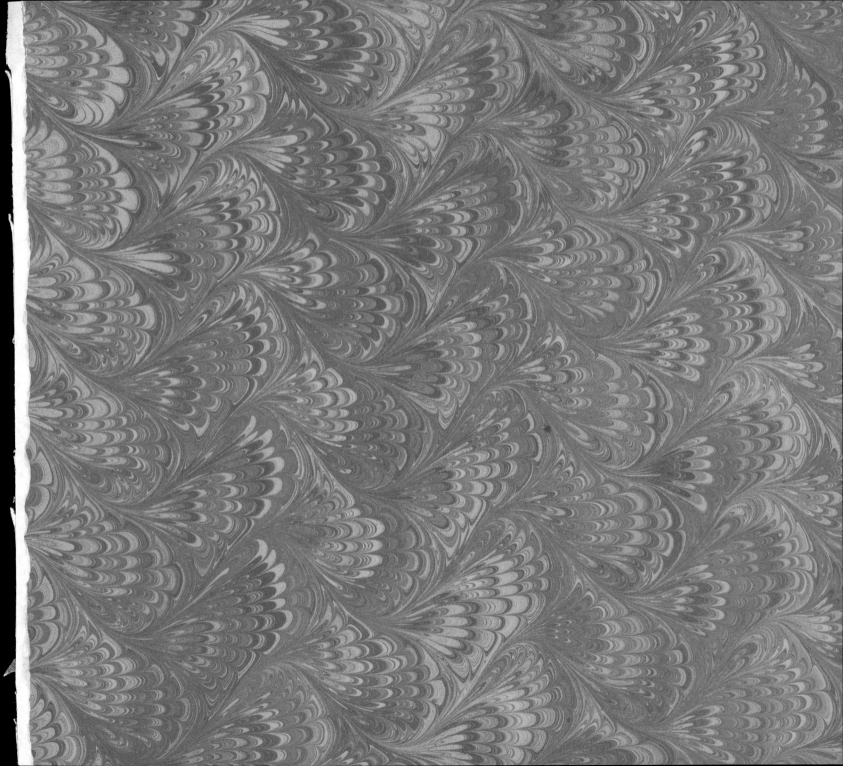